FOR ORGANS, PIANOS & ELECTRONIC KEYBOARDS

E-Z PLAY TODAY

192

65 STANDARD HITS

E-Z Play TODAY chord notation is designed for playing **standard chord positions** or **single key chords** on all **major brand organs** and **portable keyboards**.

Contents

D0783299

Cover Photo: B.A. Rubel/Shostal Assoc.

Published by
WARNER BROS. PUBLICATIONS INC.
75 Rockefeller Plaza • New York, N.Y. 10019
A Warner Communications Company

Exclusive Distributor

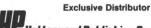
Hal Leonard Publishing Corporation
7777 West Bluemound Road P.O. Box 13819 Milwaukee, WI 53213

About A Quarter To Nine

Registration 3
Rhythm: Swing or Fox Trot

Words by Al Dubin
Music by Harry Warren

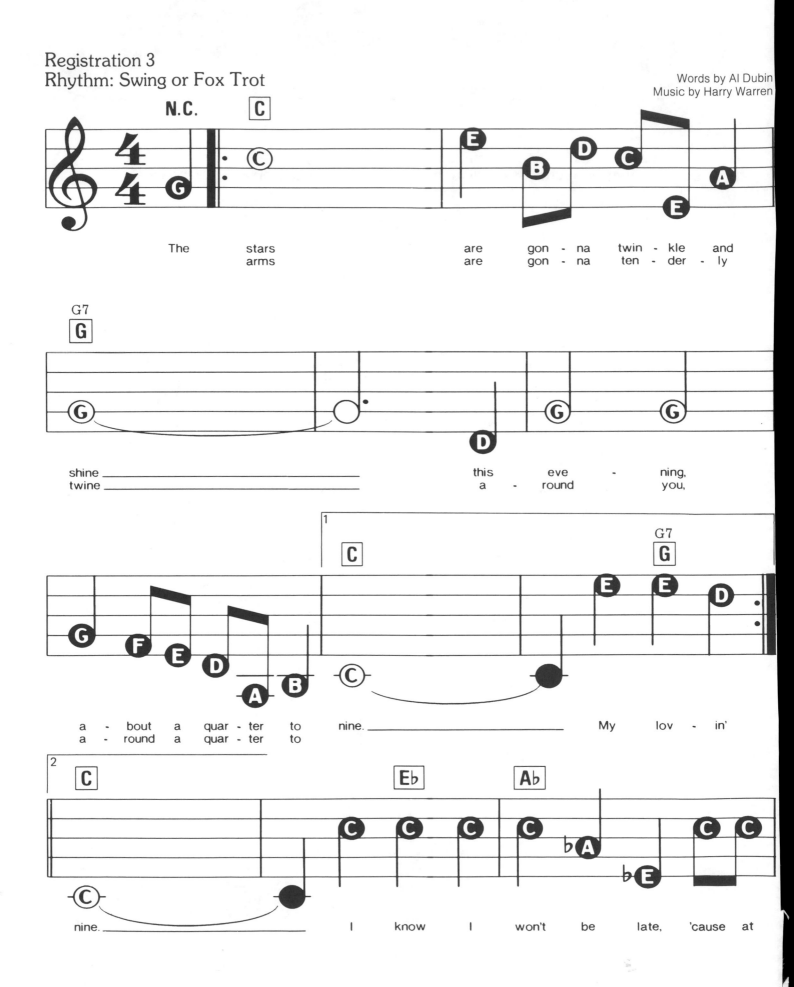

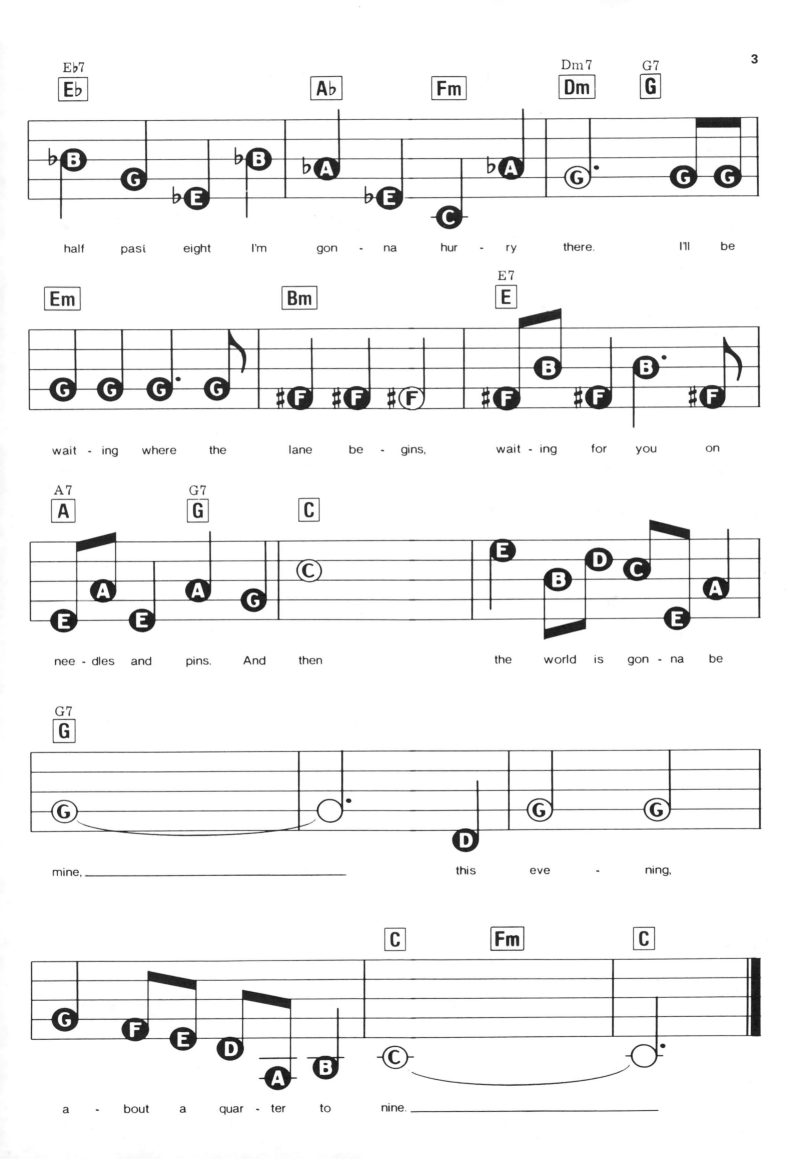

Ah! Sweet Mystery Of Life
(The Dream Melody)

Registration 3
Rhythm: Fox Trot or Ballad

Words by Rida Johnson Young
French version by Emelia Renaud
Spanish version by Johnnie Camacho
Music by Victor Herbert

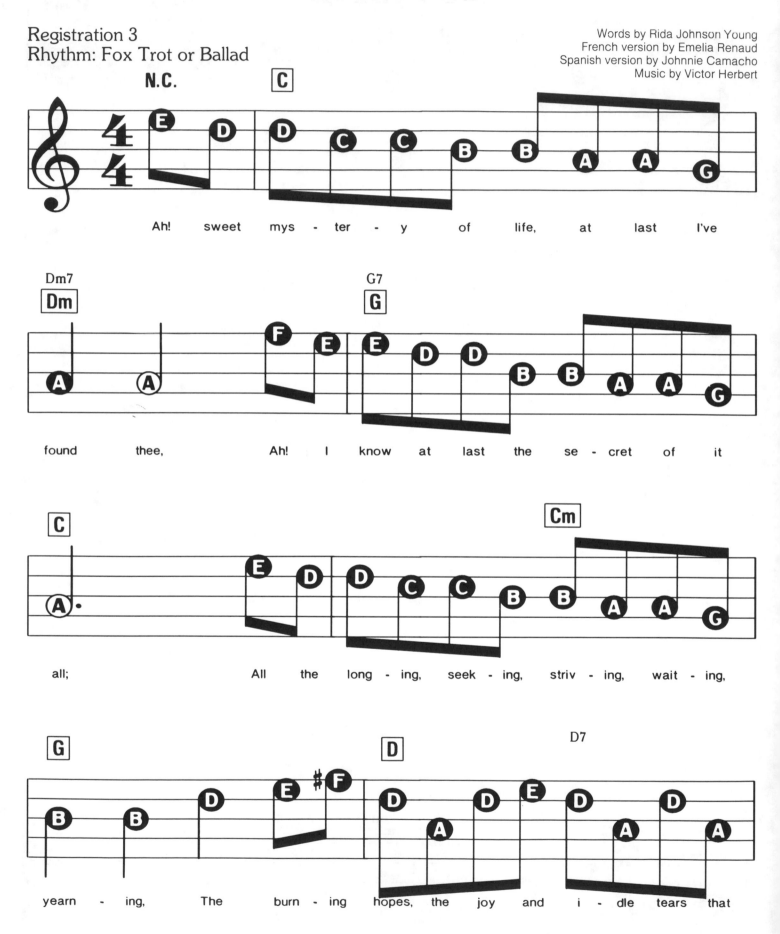

5

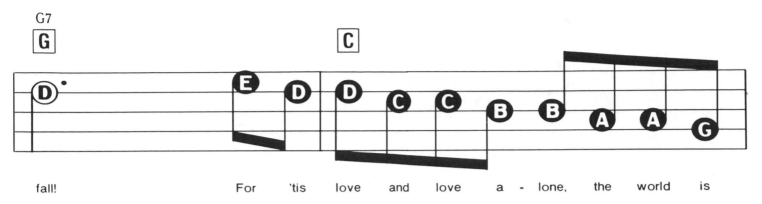

fall!   For 'tis love and love a - lone, the world is

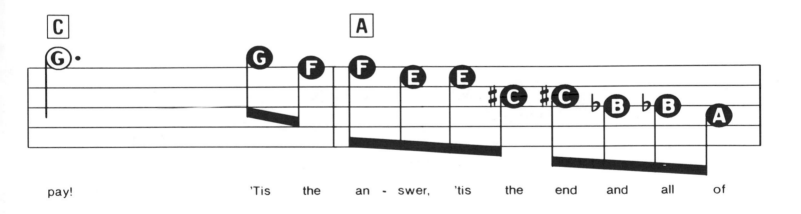

seek - ing;   And 'tis love, and love a - long, that can re-

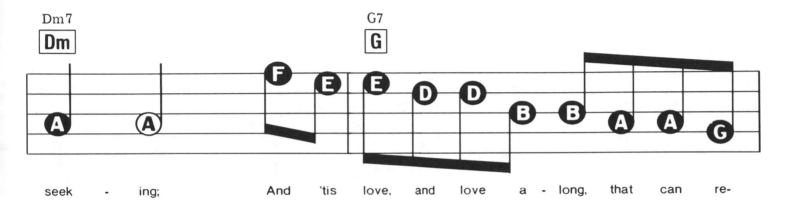

pay!   'Tis the an - swer, 'tis the end and all of

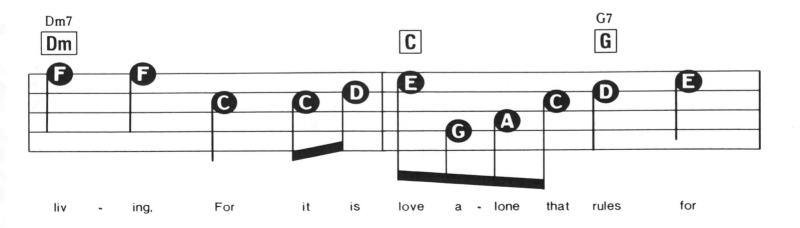

liv - ing,   For it is love a - lone that rules for

6

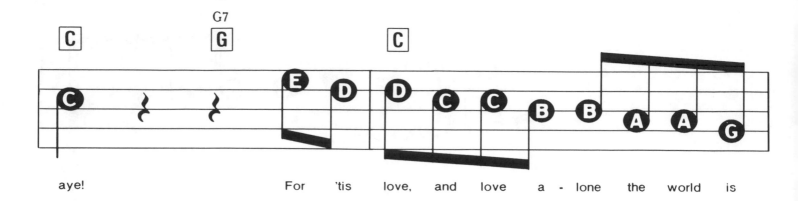

aye!   For 'tis love, and love a - lone the world is

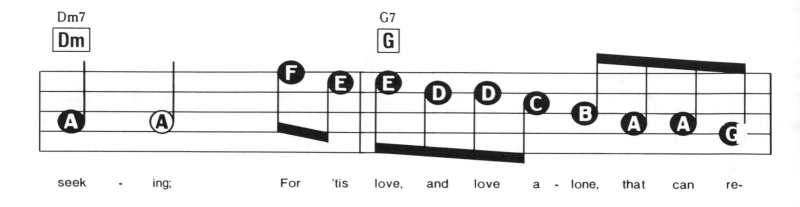

seek - ing;   For 'tis love, and love a - lone, that can re-

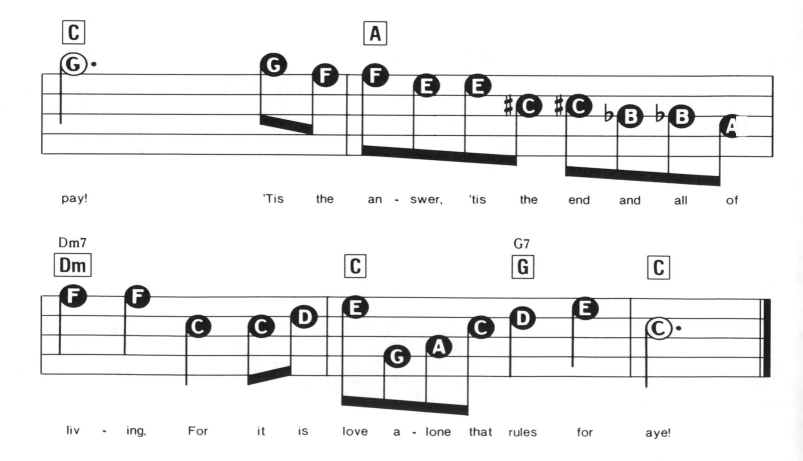

pay!   'Tis the an - swer, 'tis the end and all of

liv - ing, For it is love a - lone that rules for aye!

Begin The Beguine

Registration 2
Rhythm: Latin or Beguine

Words and Music by
Cole Porter

When they be - gin _____ the be - guine _____ it

brings back the sound _____ of mu - sic so ten - der, _____ It

brings back a night _____ of trop - i - cal splen - dour, _____ It

brings back a mem - o - ry ev - er green. _____ I'm

with you once more _____ un - der the stars _____ And

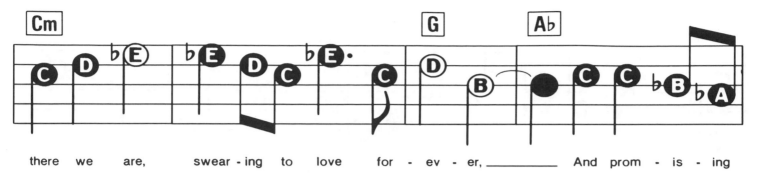

there we are, swear-ing to love for-ev-er, _____ And prom-is-ing

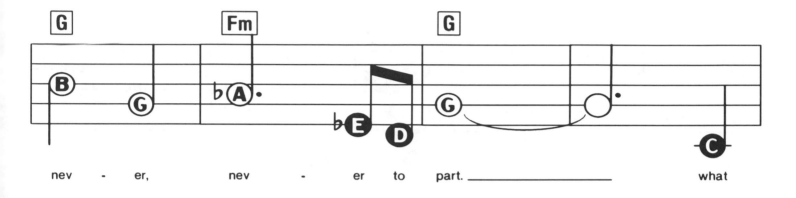

nev-er, nev-er to part. _____ what

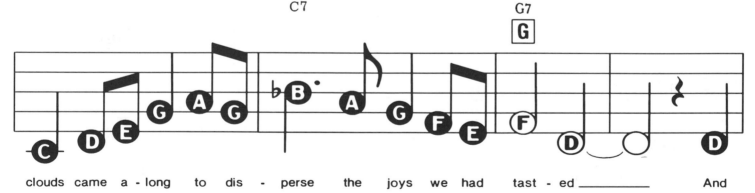

mo-ments di-vine, _____ what rap-ture se-rene, _____ Till

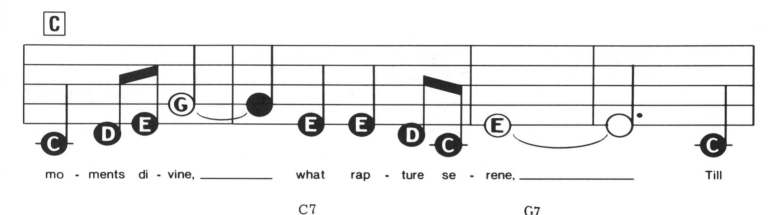

clouds came a-long to dis-perse the joys we had tast-ed _____ And

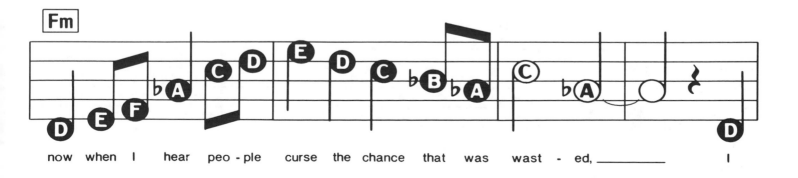

now when I hear peo-ple curse the chance that was wast-ed, _____ I

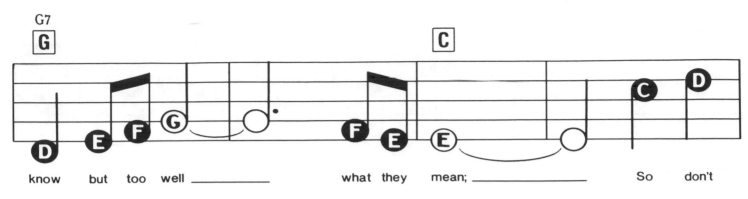

know but too well _____ what they mean; _____ So don't

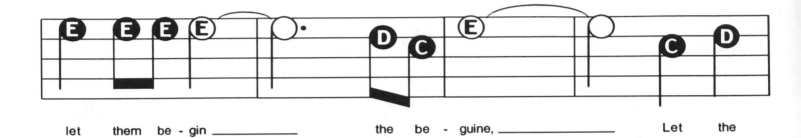

let them be - gin _____ the be - guine, _____ Let the

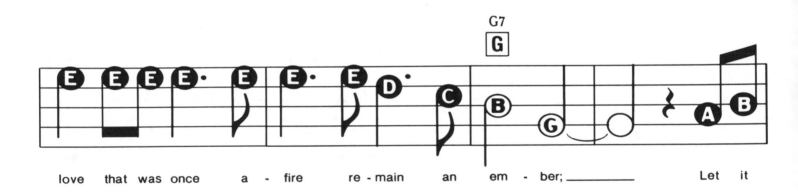

love that was once a - fire re - main an em - ber; _____ Let it

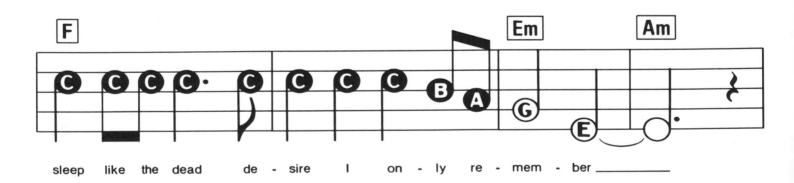

sleep like the dead de - sire I on - ly re - mem - ber _____

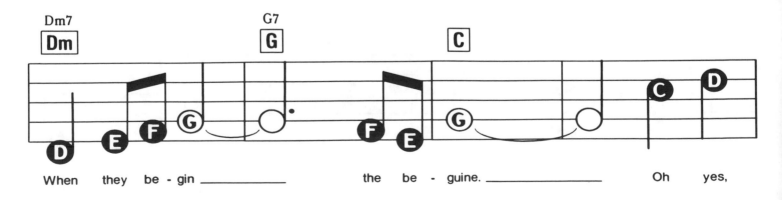

When they be - gin _____ the be - guine. _____ Oh yes,

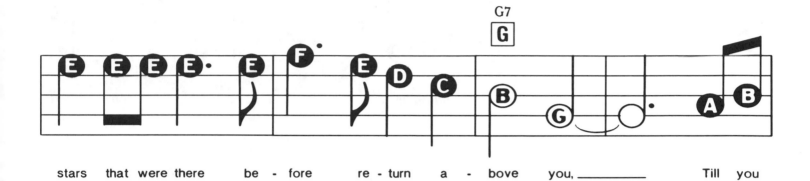

let them be - gin the be - guine, make them play _____ Till the

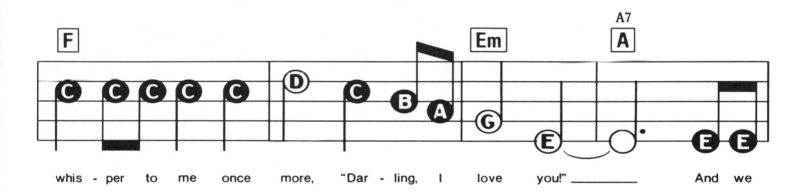

stars that were there be - fore re - turn a - bove you, _____ Till you

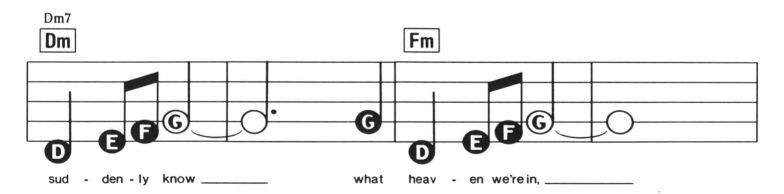

whis - per to me once more, "Dar - ling, I love you!" _____ And we

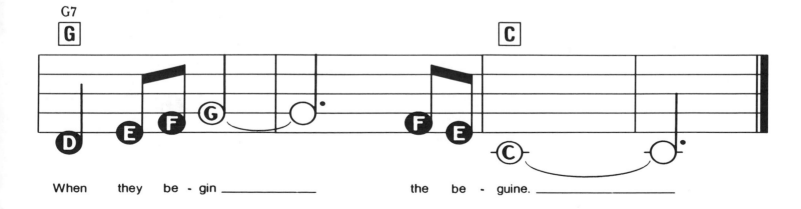

sud - den - ly know _____ what heav - en we're in, _____

When they be - gin _____ the be - guine. _____

Blow, Gabriel, Blow

Registration 4
Rhythm: Swing or Jazz

Words and Music by
Cole Porter

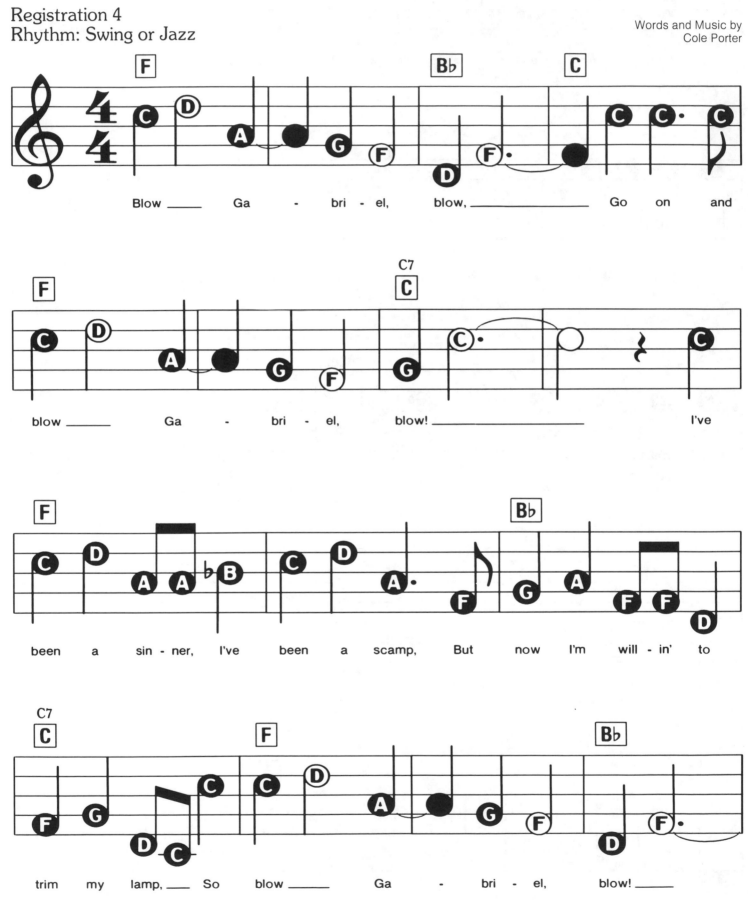

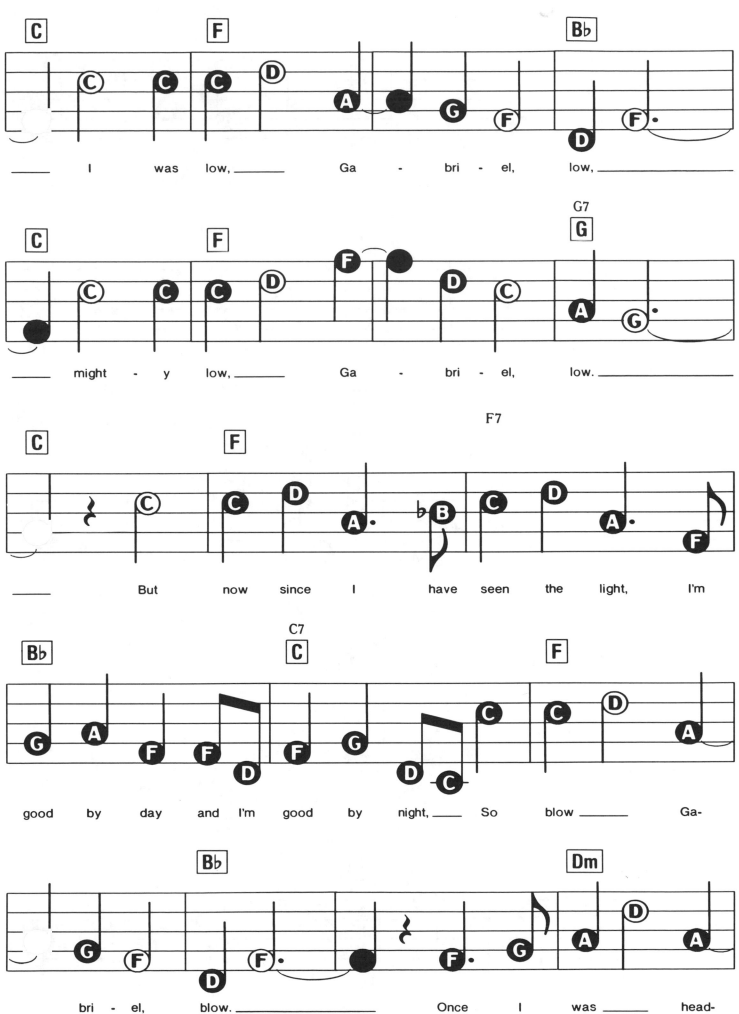

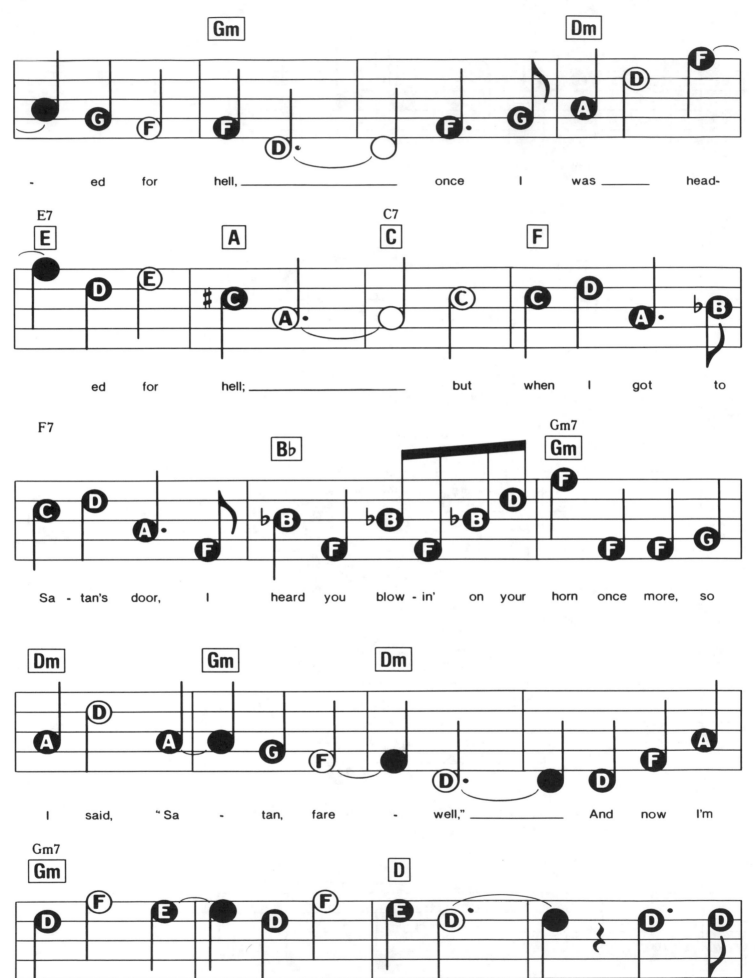

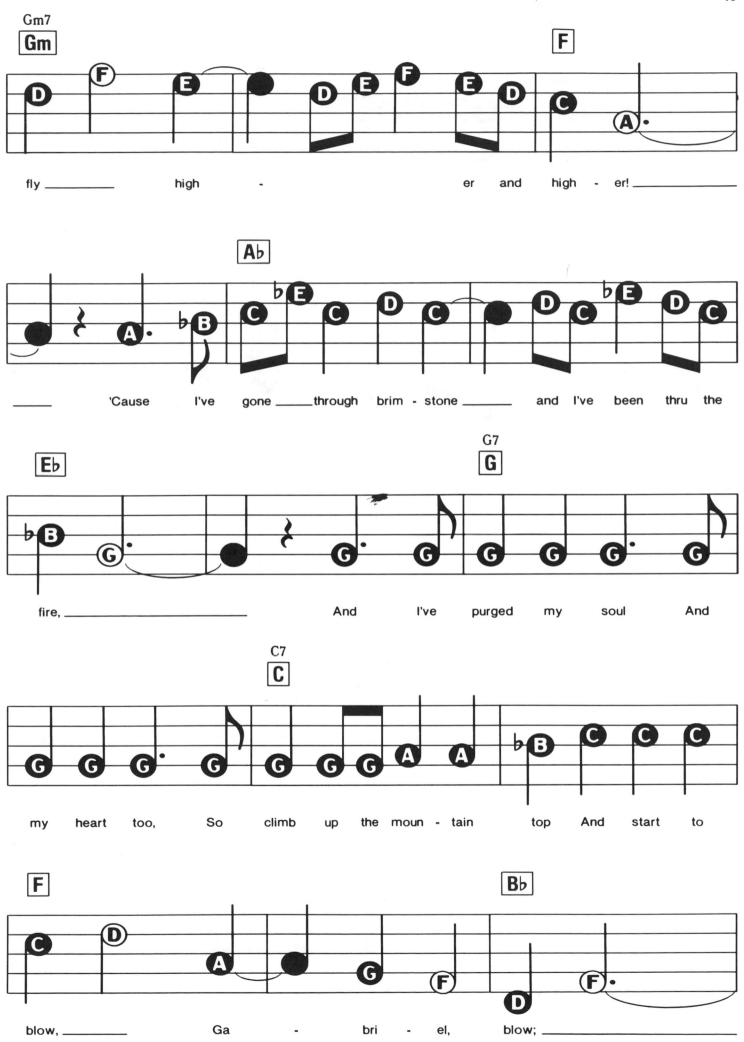

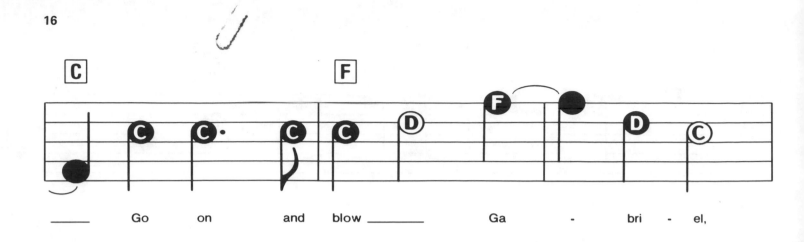

_____ Go on and blow _____ Ga - bri - el,

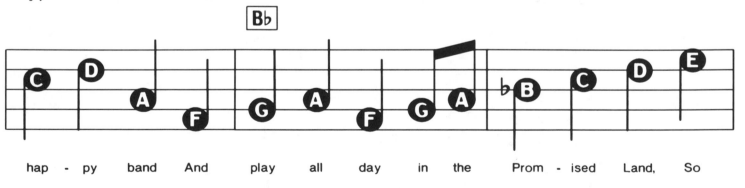

blow! _____ I want to join your

hap - py band And play all day in the Prom - ised Land, So

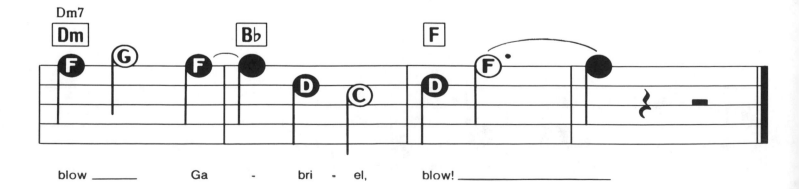

blow _____ Ga - bri - el, blow! _____

Blues In The Night
(My Mama Done Tol' Me)

Registration 7
Rhythm: Swing or Jazz

Words by Johnny Mercer
Music by Harold Arlen

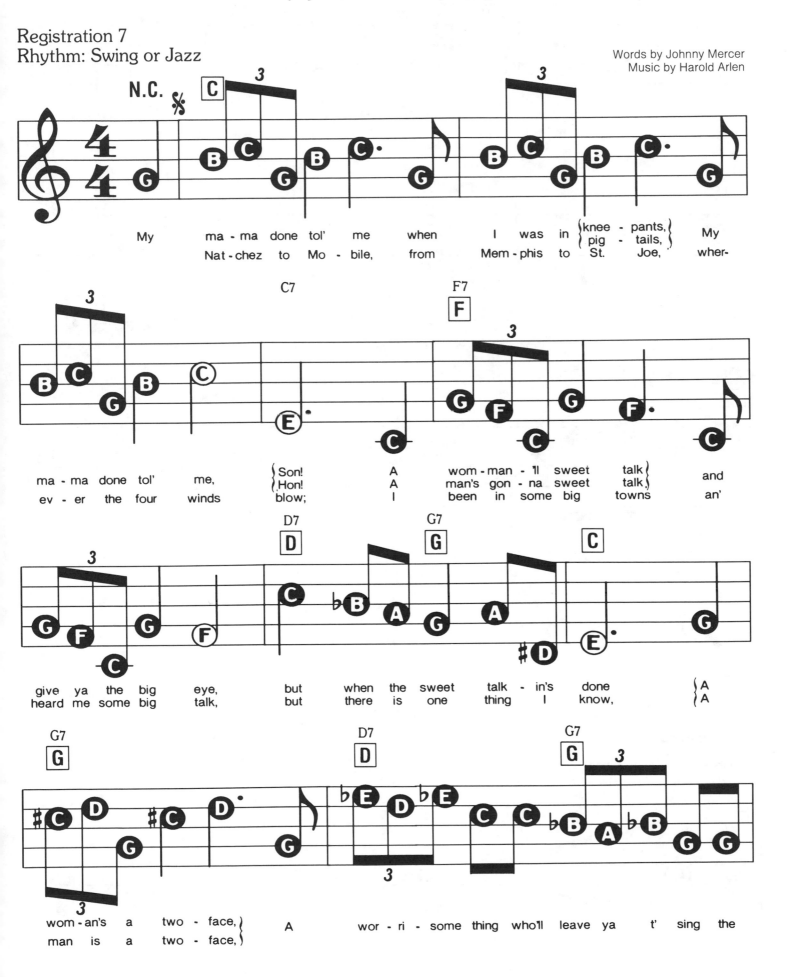

18

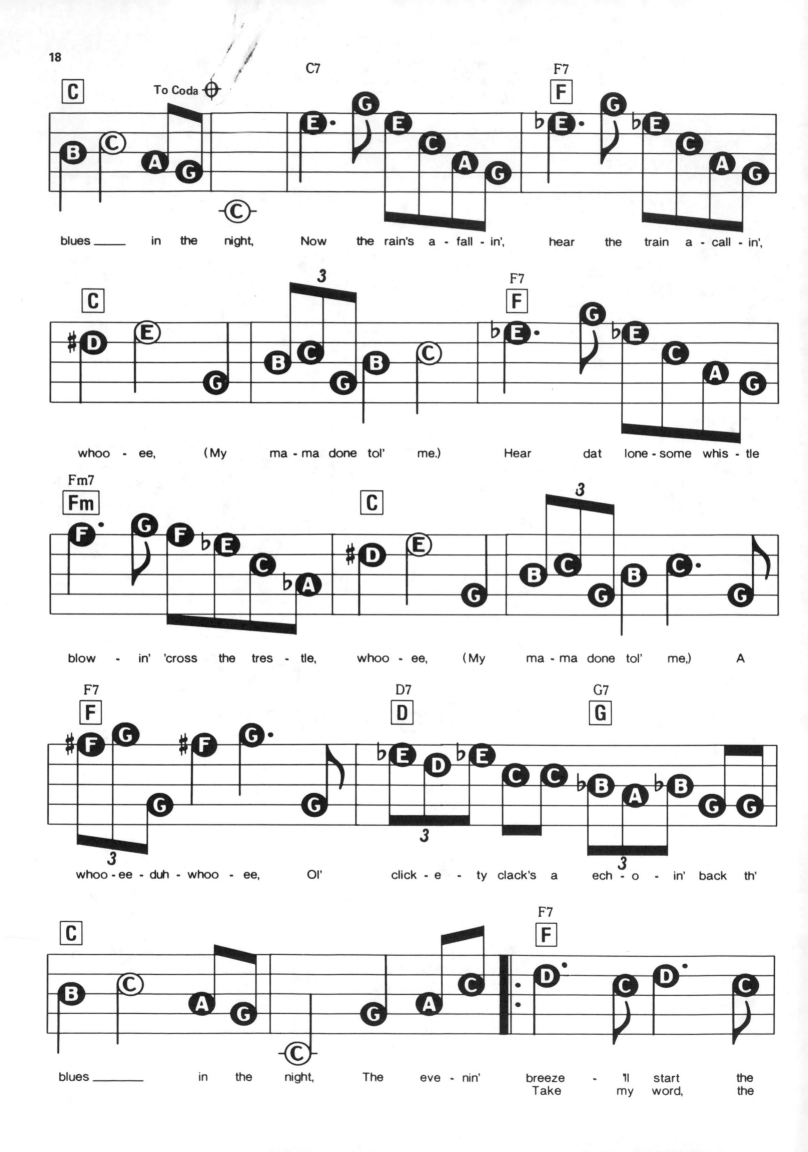

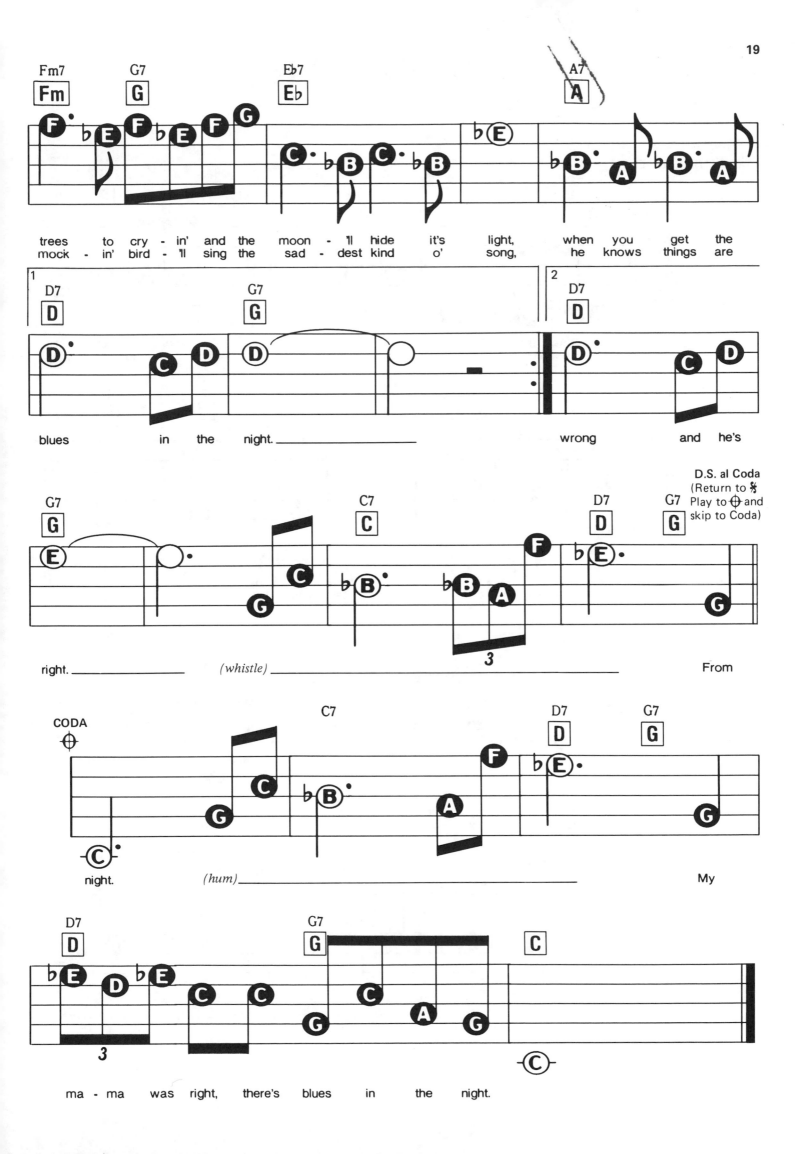

Body And Soul

Words by Edward Heyman, Robert Sour
and Frank Eyton
Music by John Green

Registration 4
Rhythm: Ballad

Brian's Song
(Theme from the Screen Gems T.V. Production "Brian's Song")

Registration 10
Rhythm: Slow Rock or Ballad

Music by Michel Legrand

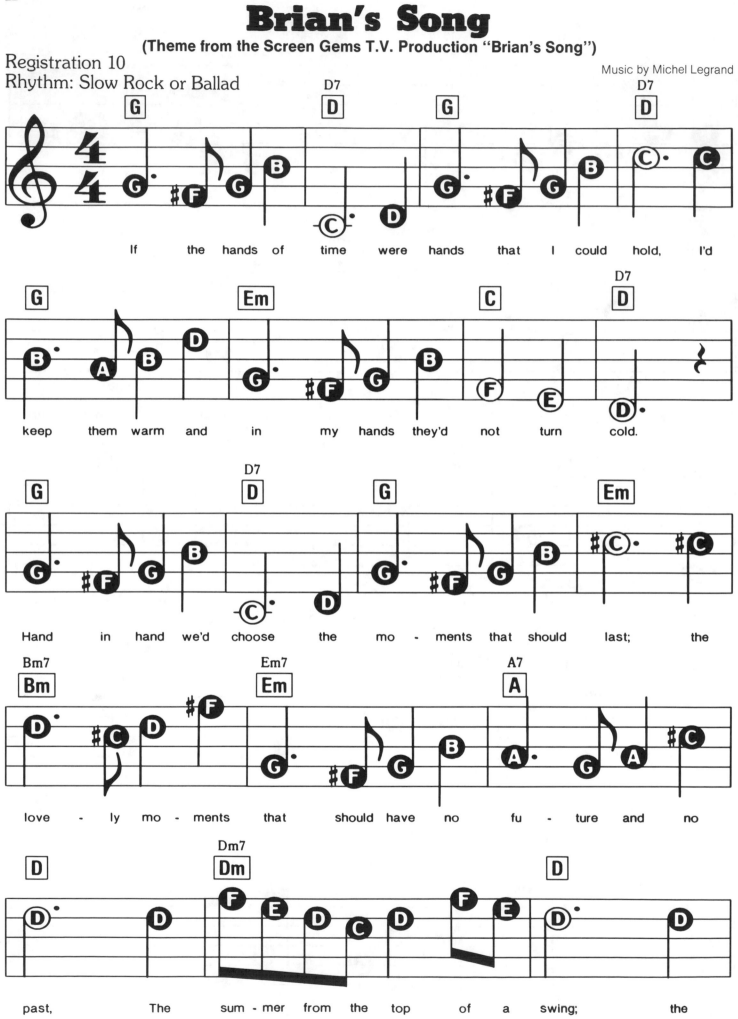

If the hands of time were hands that I could hold, I'd

keep them warm and in my hands they'd not turn cold.

Hand in hand we'd choose the mo - ments that should last; the

love - ly mo - ments that should have no fu - ture and no

past, The sum - mer from the top of a swing; the

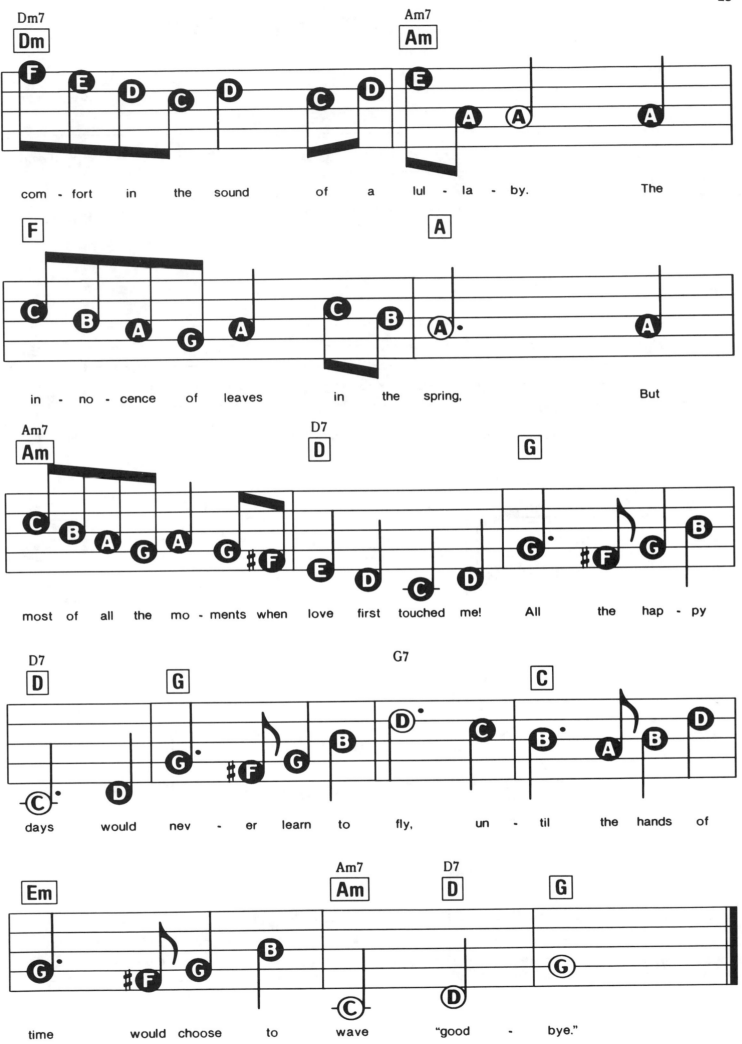

Cheerful Little Earful

Registration 8
Rhythm: Fox Trot or Swing

Words by Ira Gershwin and Billy Rose
Music by Harry Warren

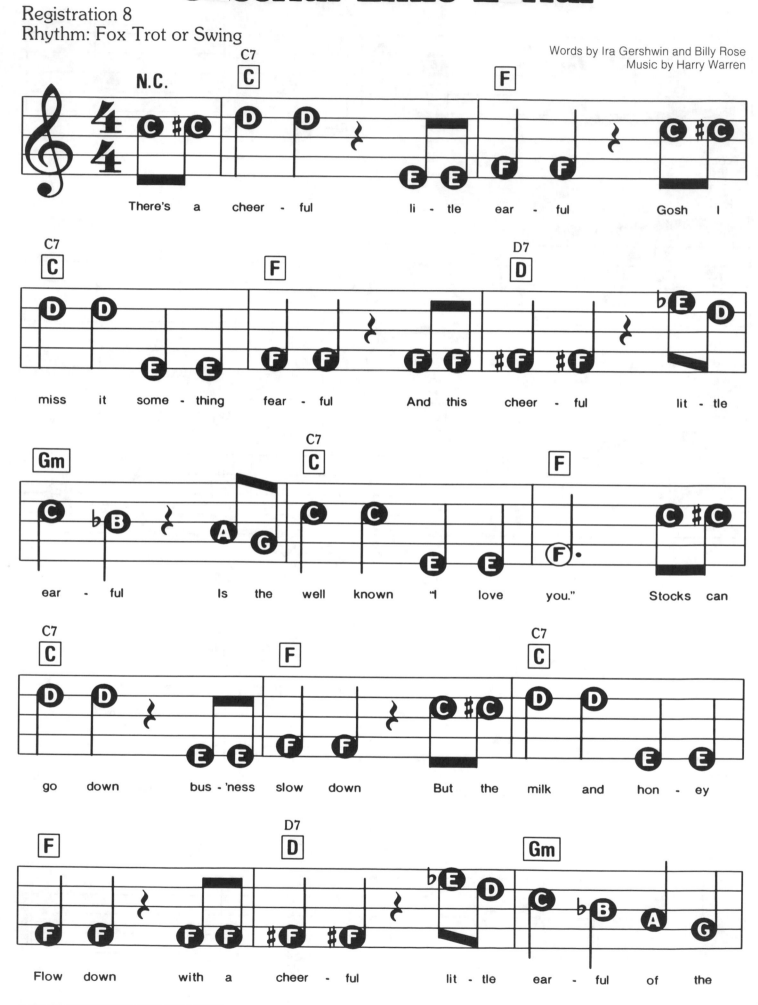

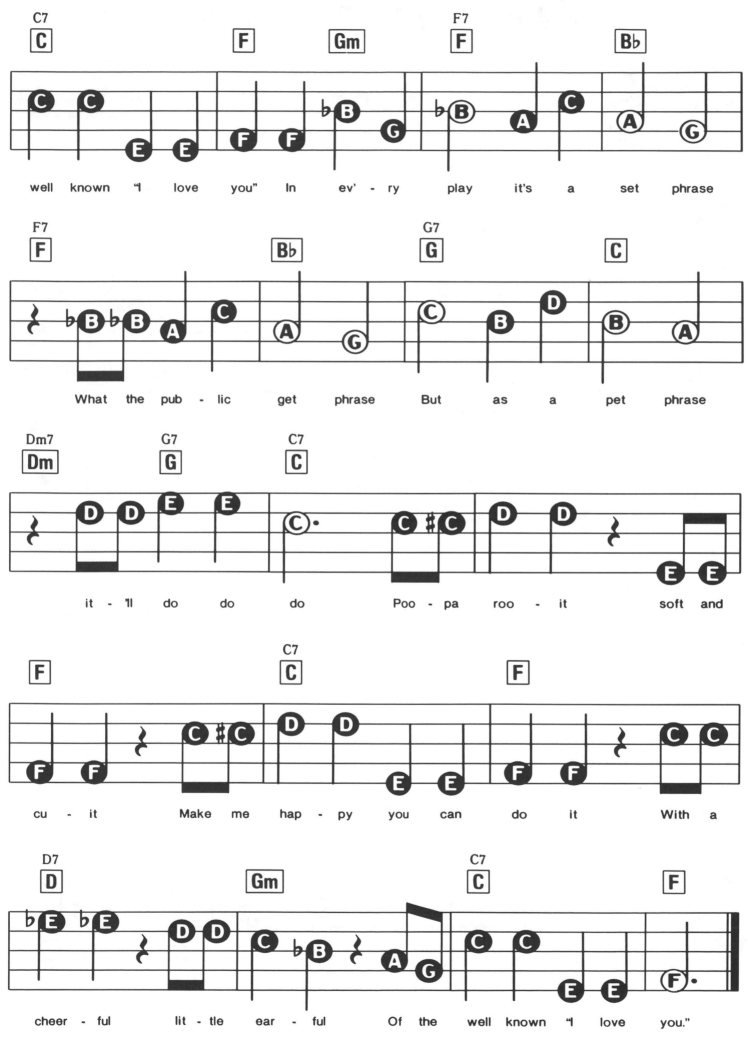

Dancing In The Dark

Registration 3
Rhythm: Fox Trot or Swing

Words by Howard Dietz
Music by Arthur Schwartz

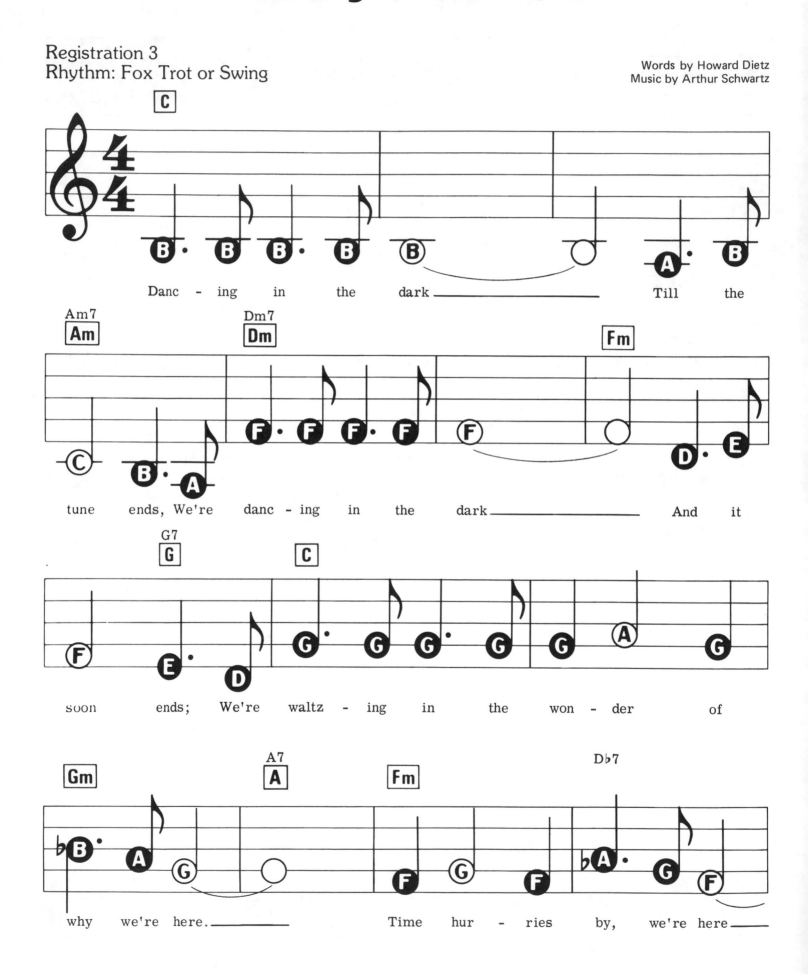

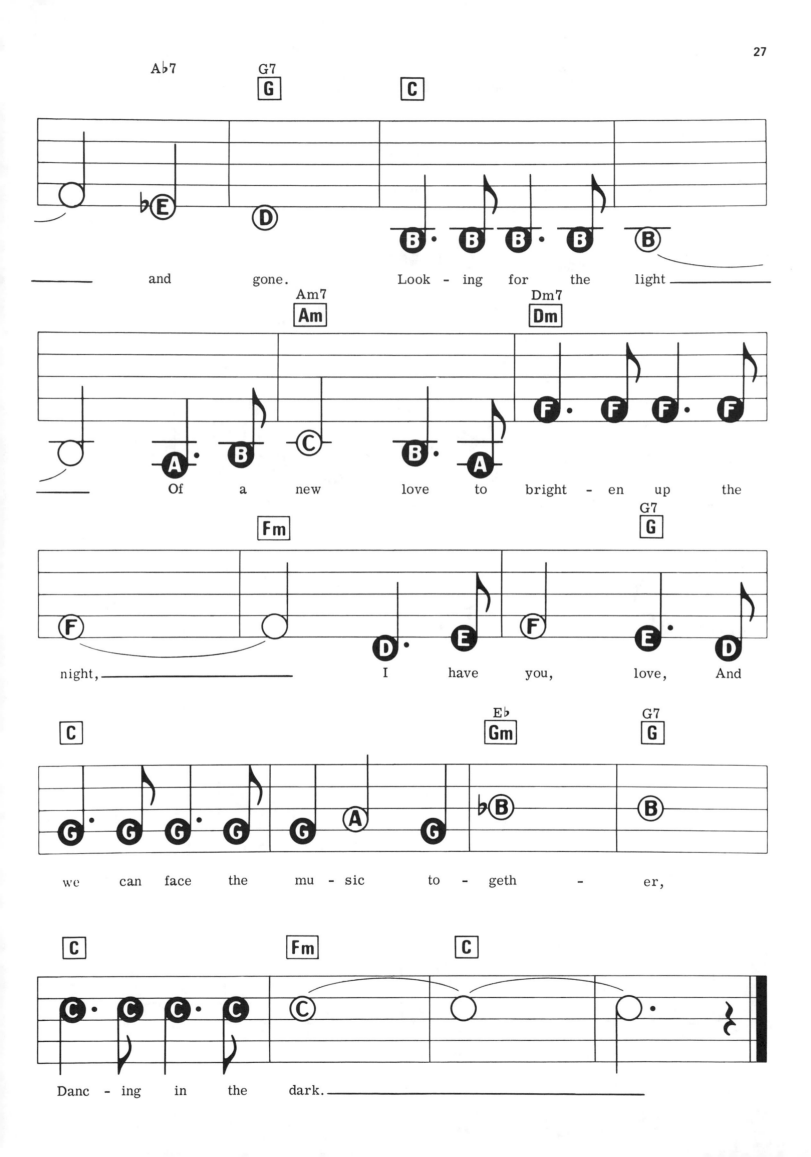

Danke Schoen

Registration 9
Rhythm: Swing

Words by Kurt Schwabach and Milt Gabler
Music by Bert Kaempfert

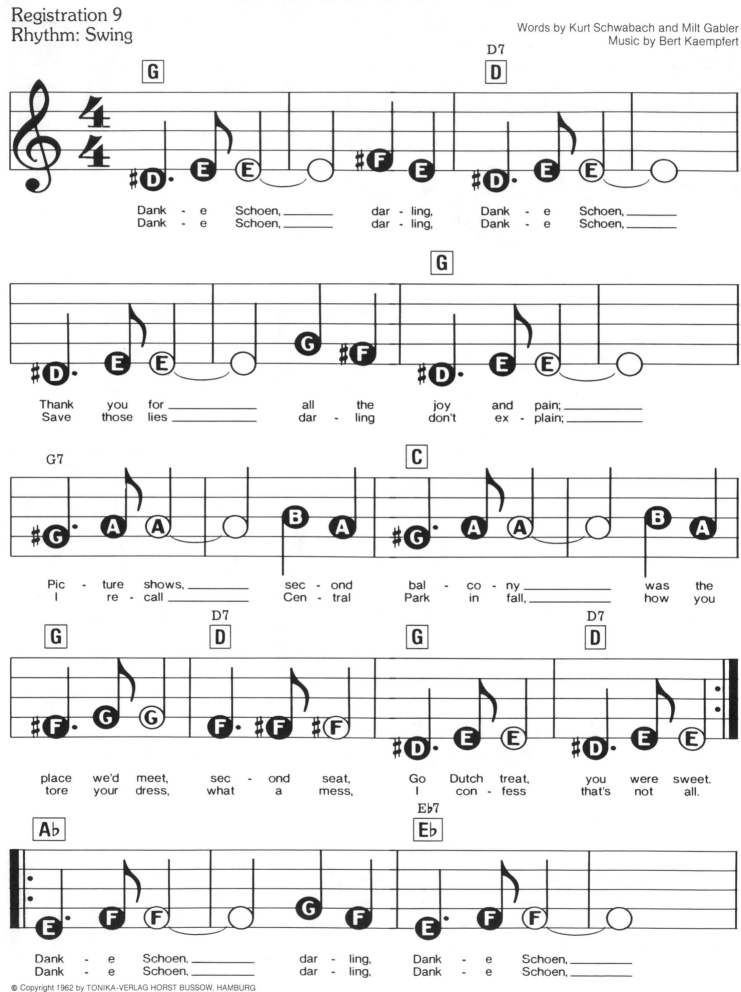

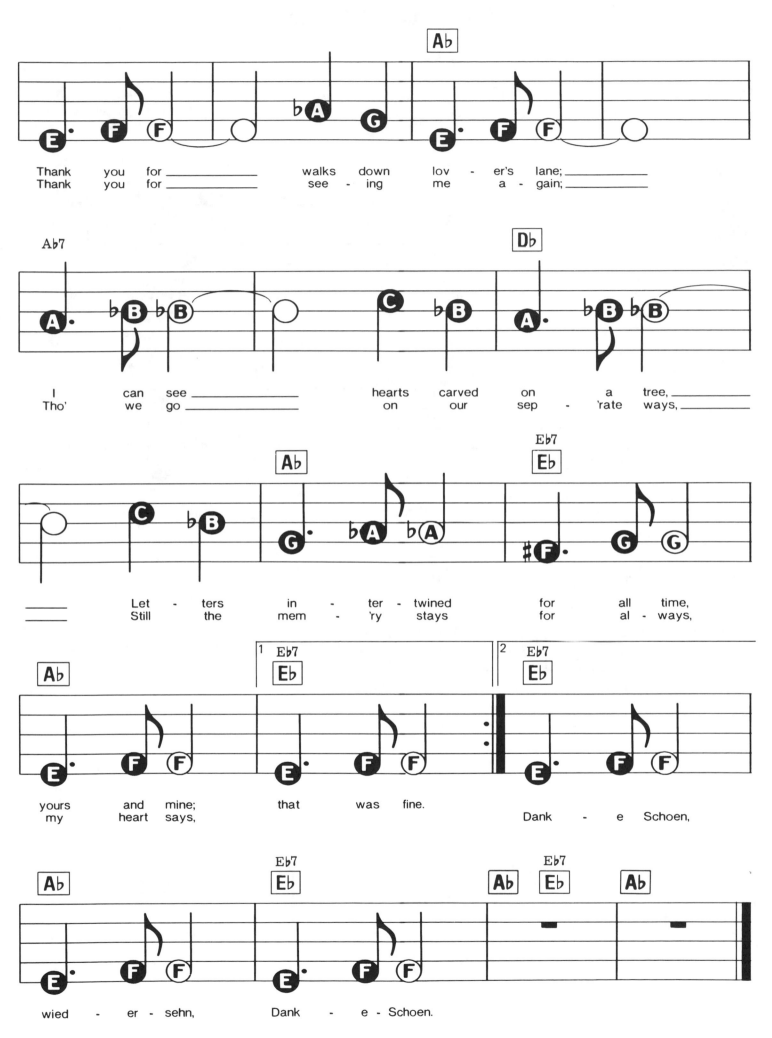

Deep Night

Registration 5
Rhythm: Fox Trot or Swing

Words by Rudy Vallee
Music by Charlie Henderson

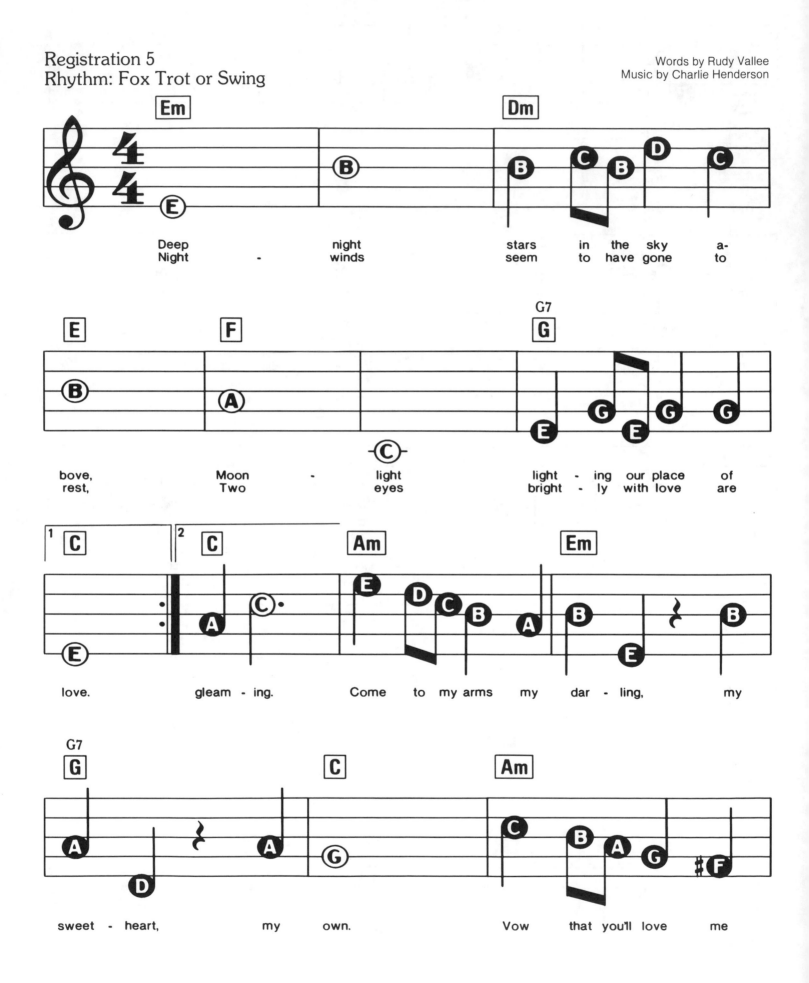

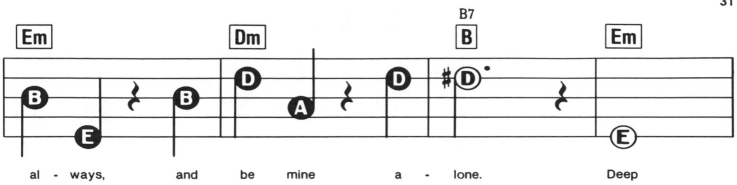

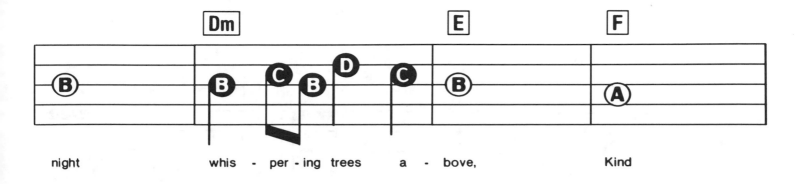

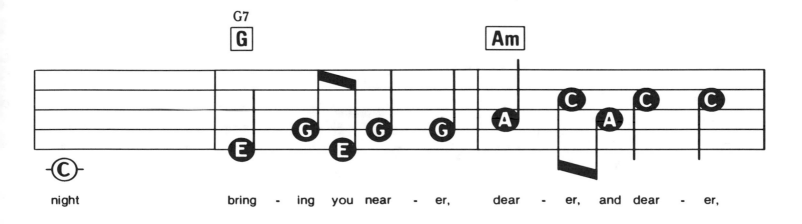

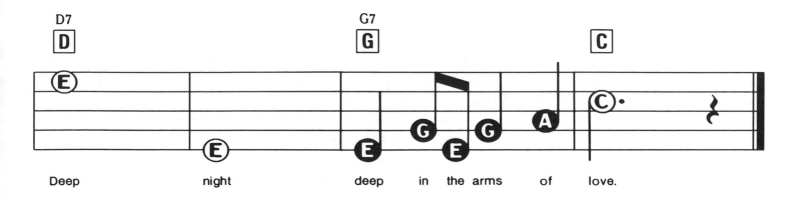

Delicado
(Baiao)

Registration 3
Rhythm: Latin or Tango

Words by Jack Lawrence
Music by Waldyr Azevedo

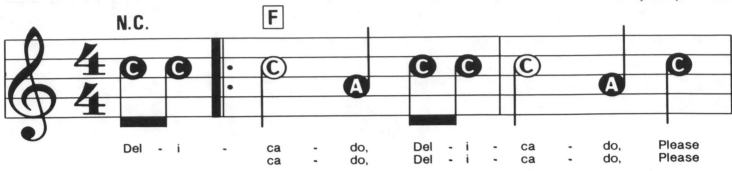

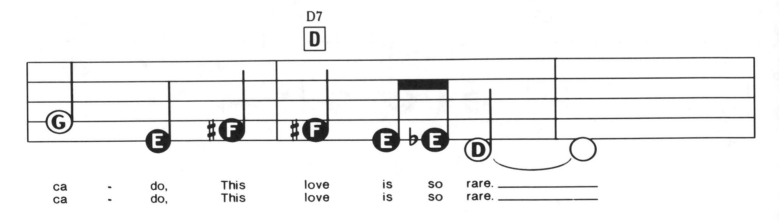

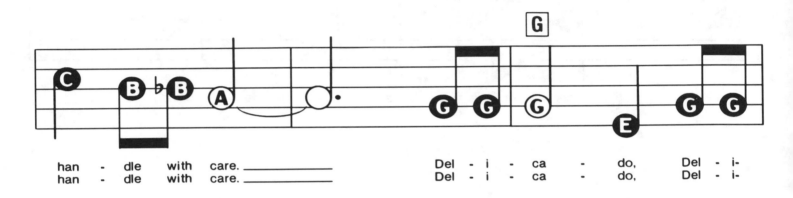

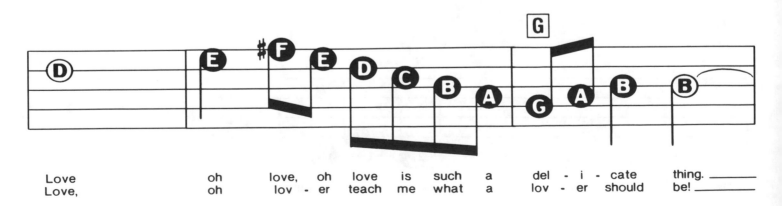

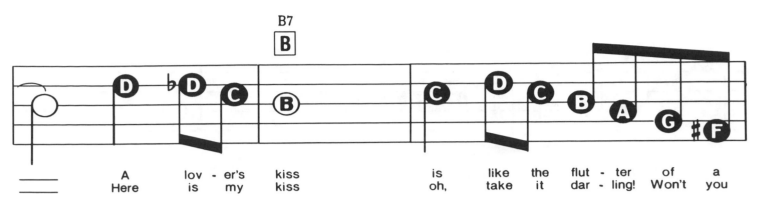

A lov - er's kiss   is, like the flut - ter of a
Here is my kiss   oh, take it dar - ling! Won't you

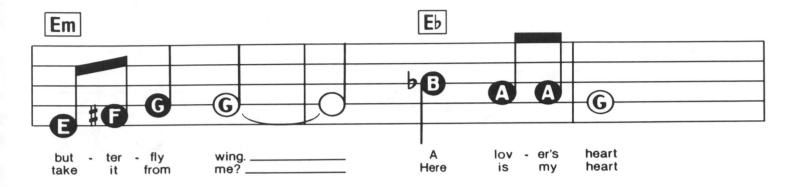

but - ter - fly   wing. _____   A lov - er's heart
take it from   me? _____   Here is my heart

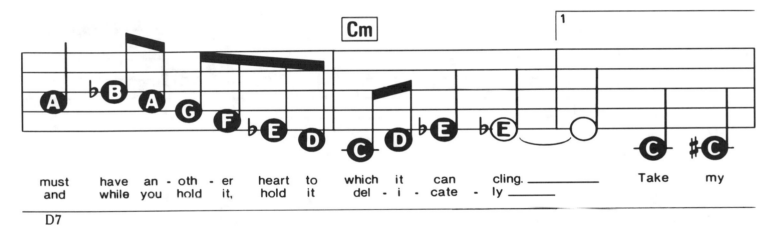

must have an - oth - er heart to which it can cling. _____   Take my
and while you hold it, hold it del - i - cate - ly _____

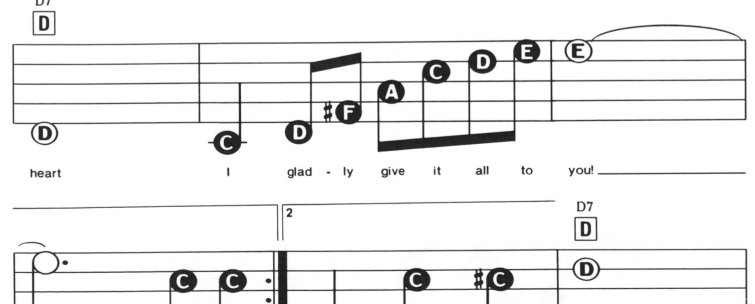

heart   I glad - ly give it all to you! _____

____   Del - i - ____   Take my heart

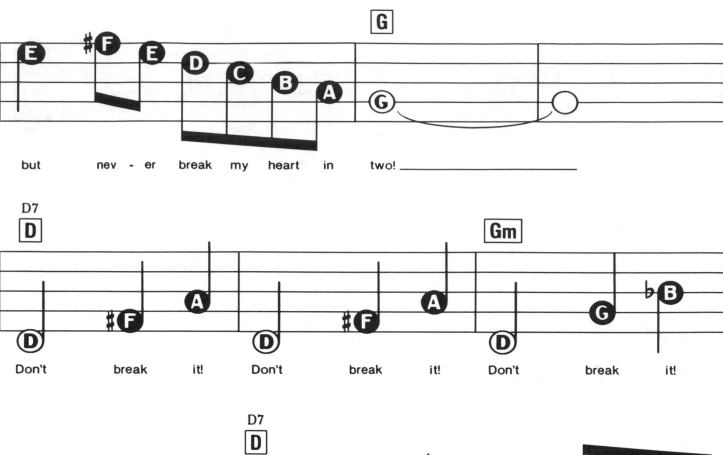

but   nev - er   break   my   heart   in   two! _____

Don't   break   it!   Don't   break   it!   Don't   break   it!

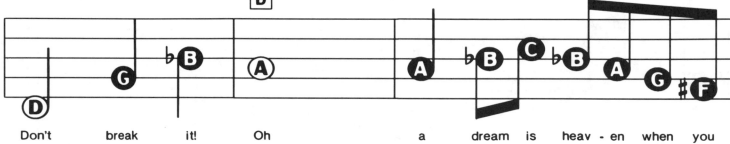

Don't   break   it!   Oh   a   dream   is   heav - en   when   you

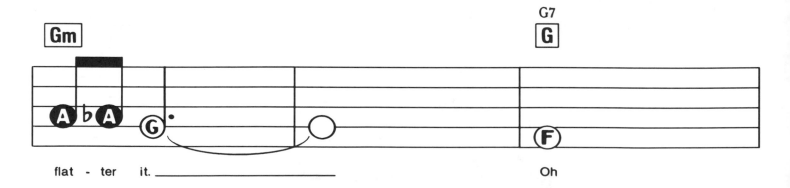

flat - ter   it. _____   Oh

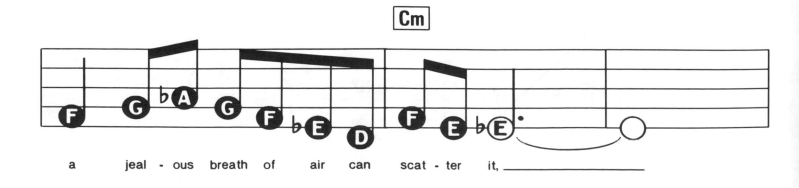

a   jeal - ous   breath   of   air   can   scat - ter   it, _____

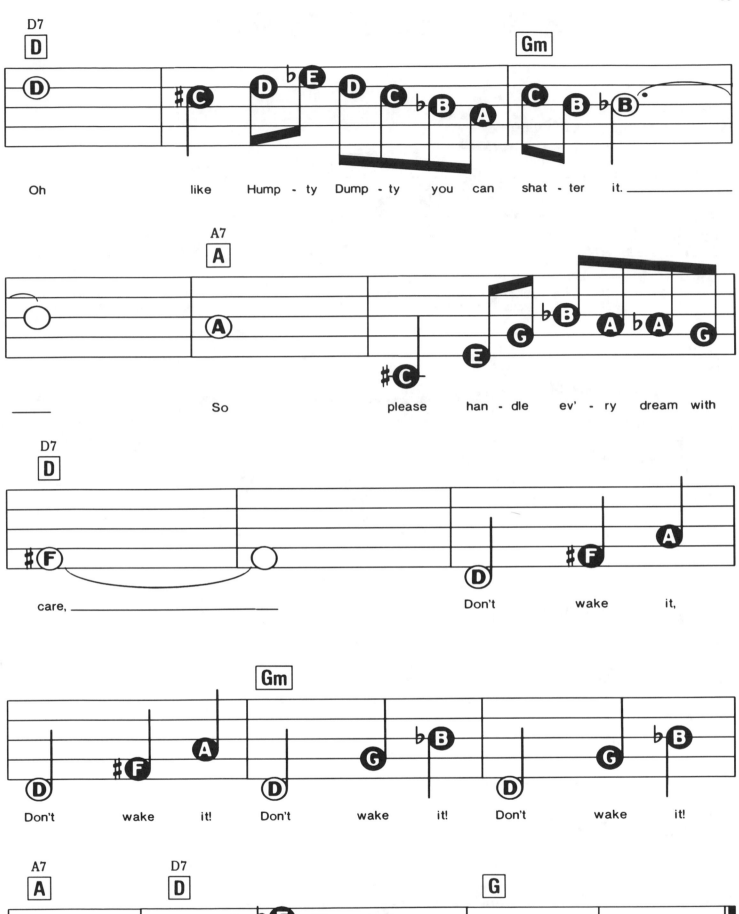

Oh   like Hump-ty Dump-ty you can shat-ter it. _____

_____   So   please han-dle ev'-ry dream with

care, _____   Don't   wake   it,

Don't   wake   it! Don't   wake   it! Don't   wake   it!

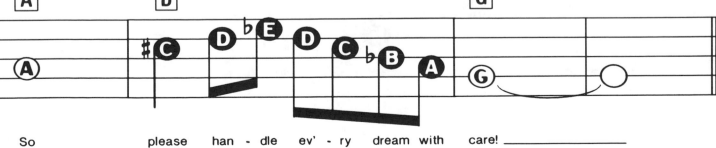

So   please han-dle ev'-ry dream with care! _____

A Dreamer's Holiday

Registration 4
Rhythm: Fox Trot or Swing

Words by Kim Gannon
Music by Mabel Wayne

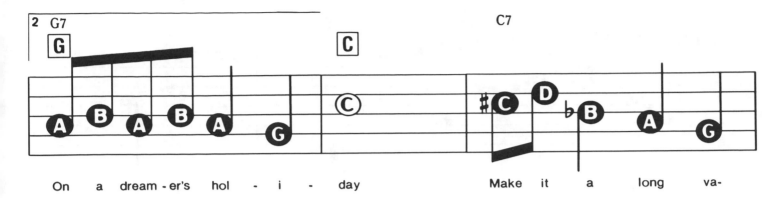

On a dream-er's hol - i - day   Make it a long va-

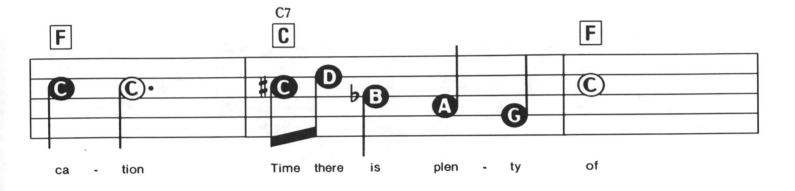

ca - tion   Time there is plen - ty of

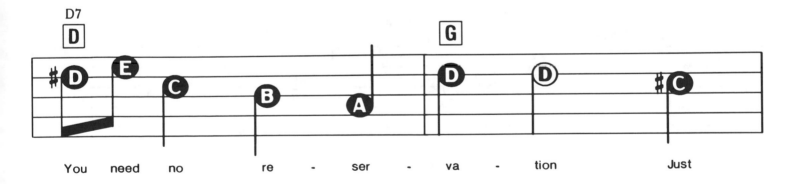

You need no re - ser - va - tion   Just

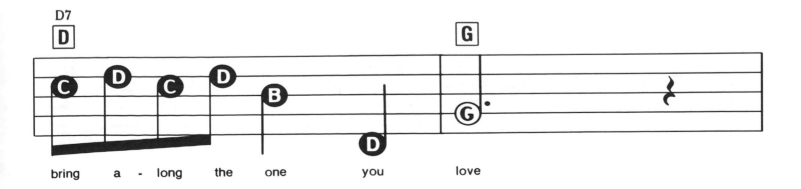

bring a - long the one you love

38

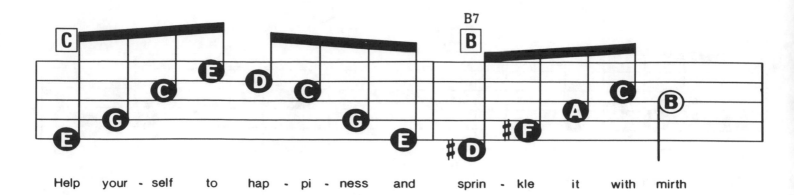

Help your - self to hap - pi - ness and sprin - kle it with mirth

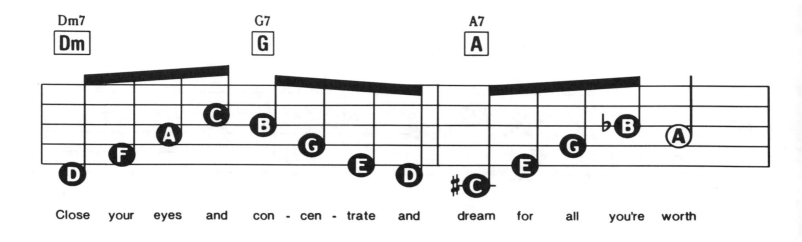

Close your eyes and con - cen - trate and dream for all you're worth

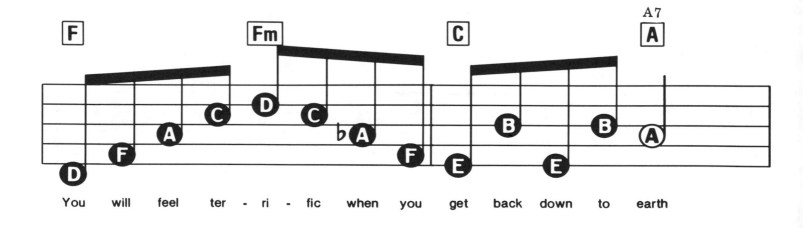

You will feel ter - ri - fic when you get back down to earth

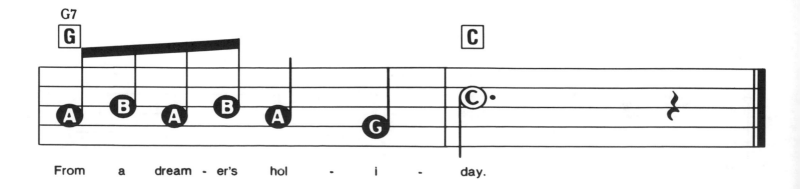

From a dream - er's hol - i - day.

Drinking Song

Registration 3
Rhythm: Waltz

Words by Dorothy Donnelly
Music by Sigmund Romberg

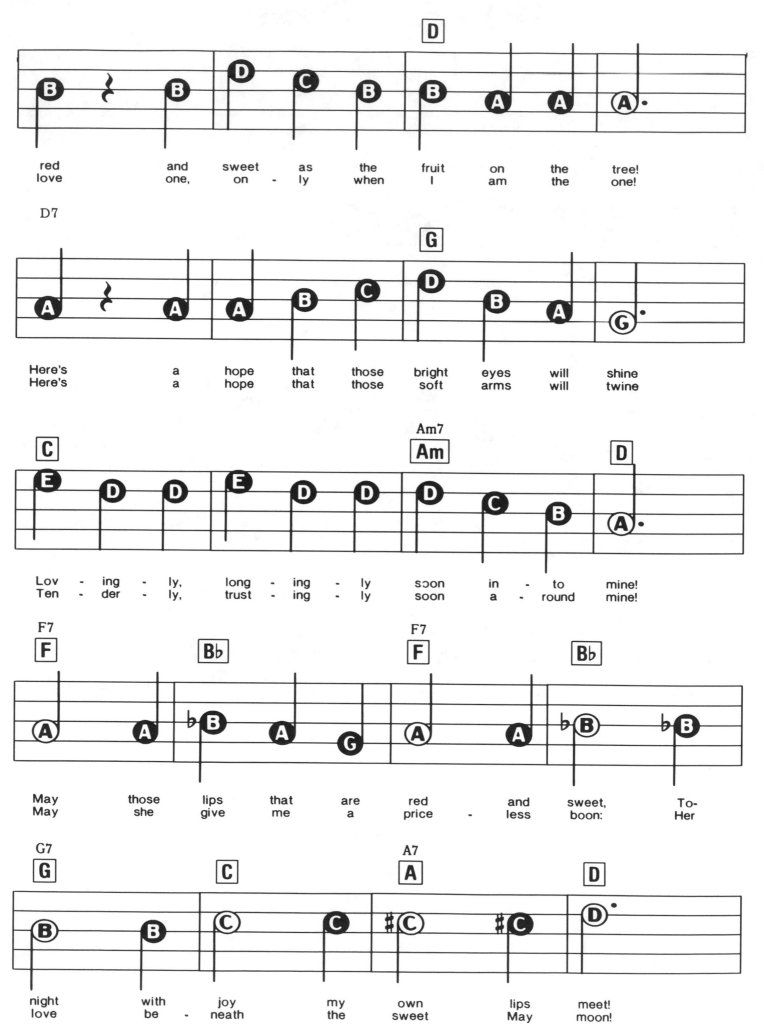

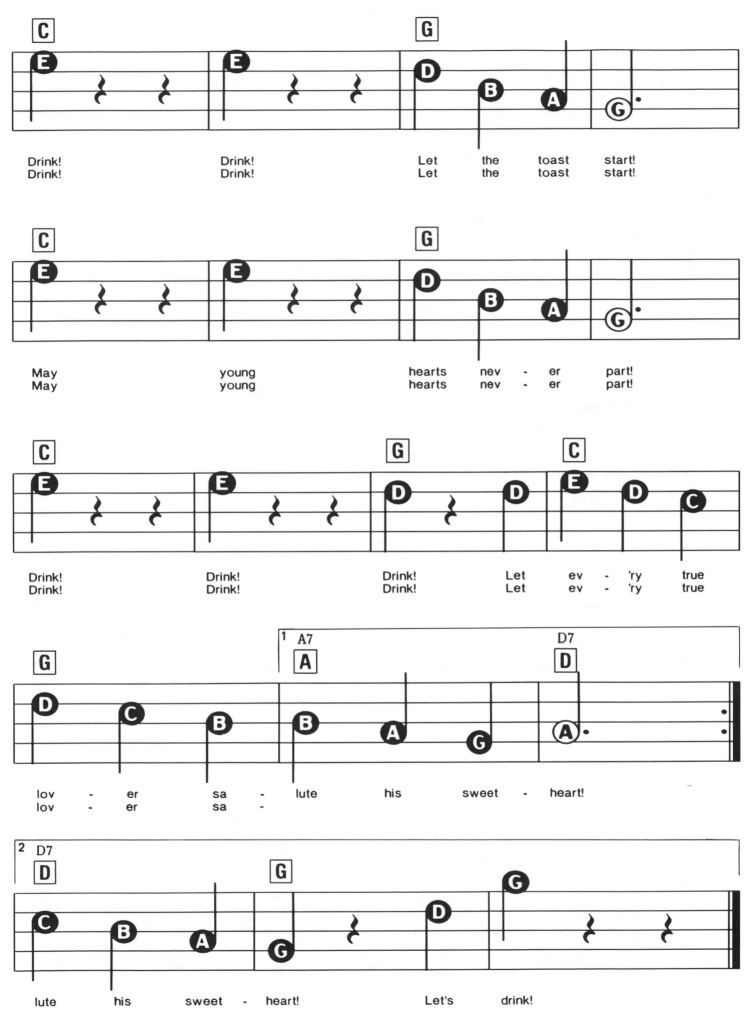

Early Autumn

Registration 7
Rhythm: Fox Trot or Ballad

Words by Johnny Mercer
Music by Ralph Burns and Woody Herman

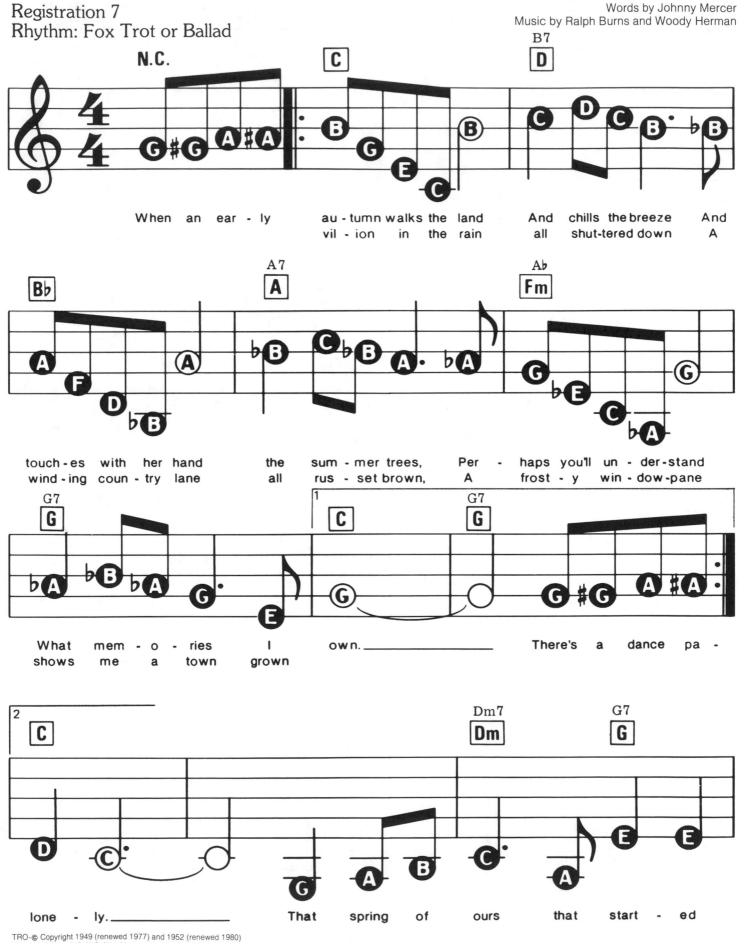

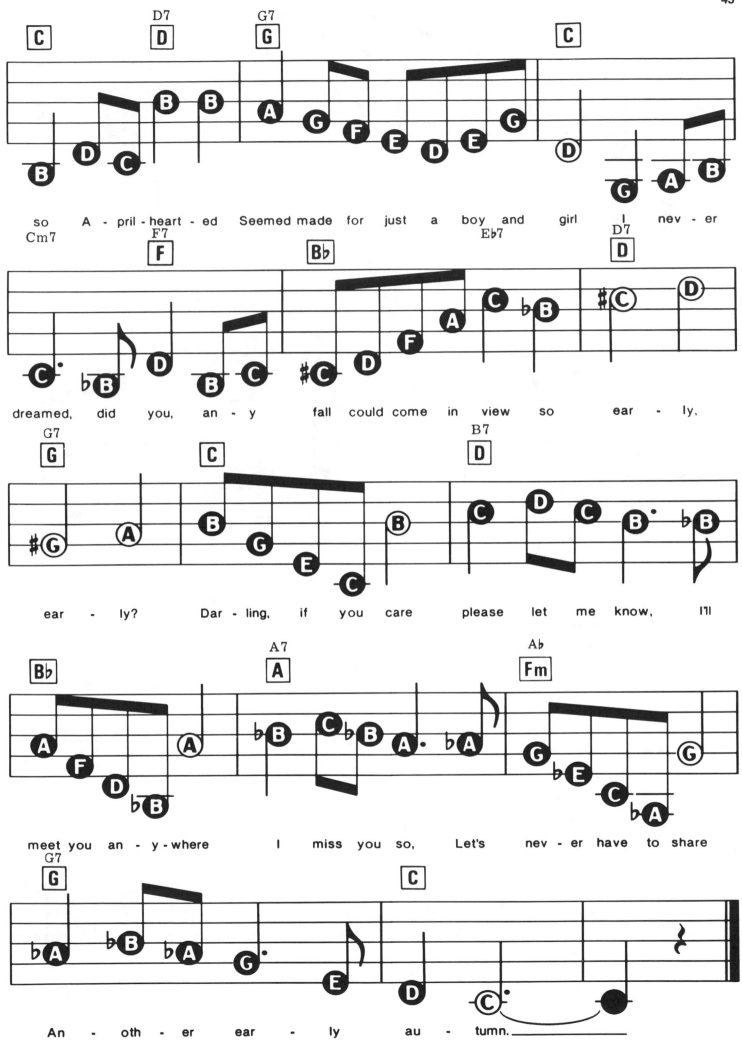

Fools Rush In
(Where Angels Fear To Tread)

Registration 9
Rhythm: Fox Trot or Ballad

Words by Johnny Mercer
Music by Rube Bloom

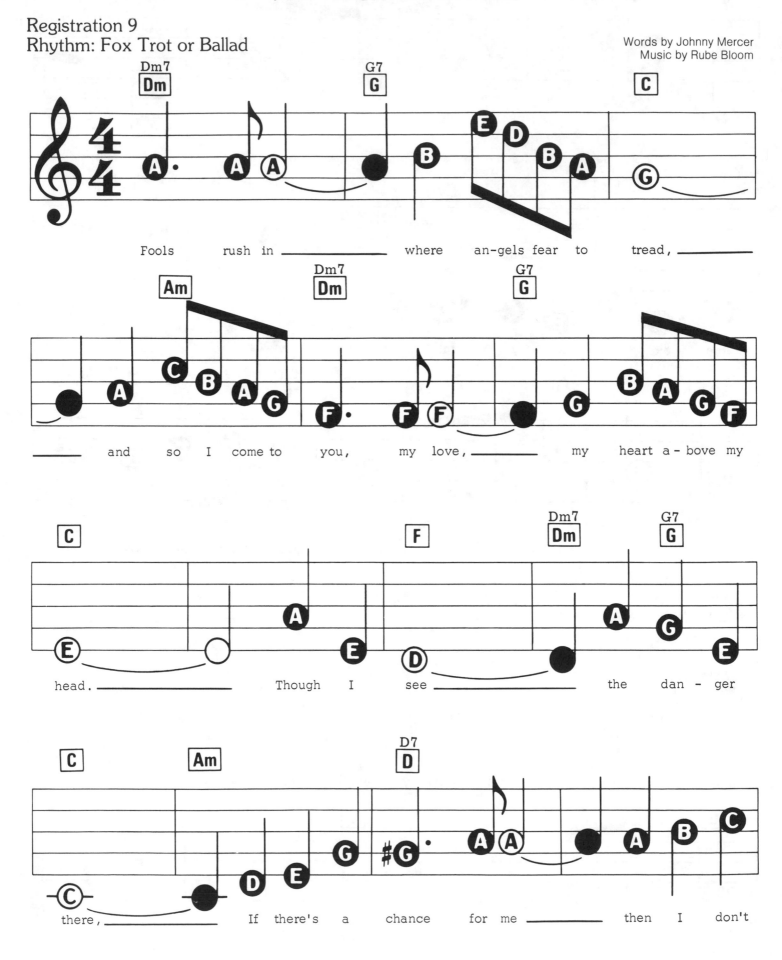

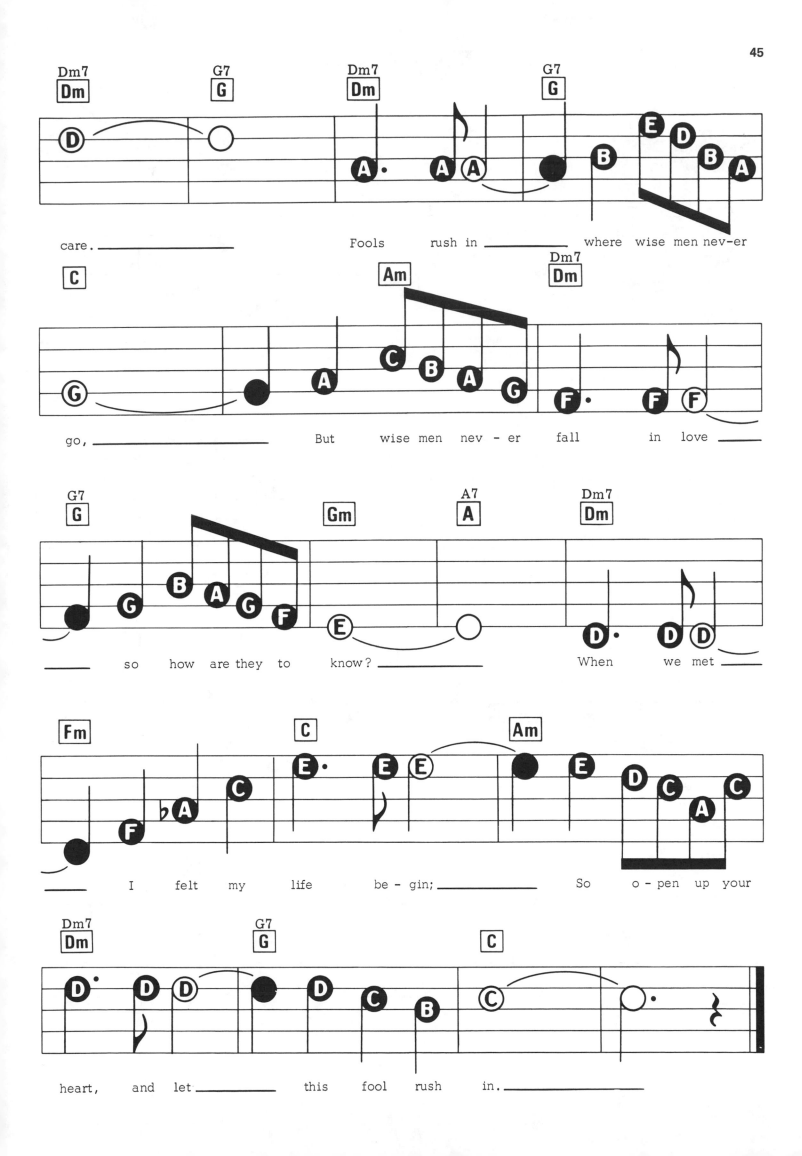

For You

Words by Al Dubin
Music by Harry Warren

Registration 2
Rhythm: Waltz

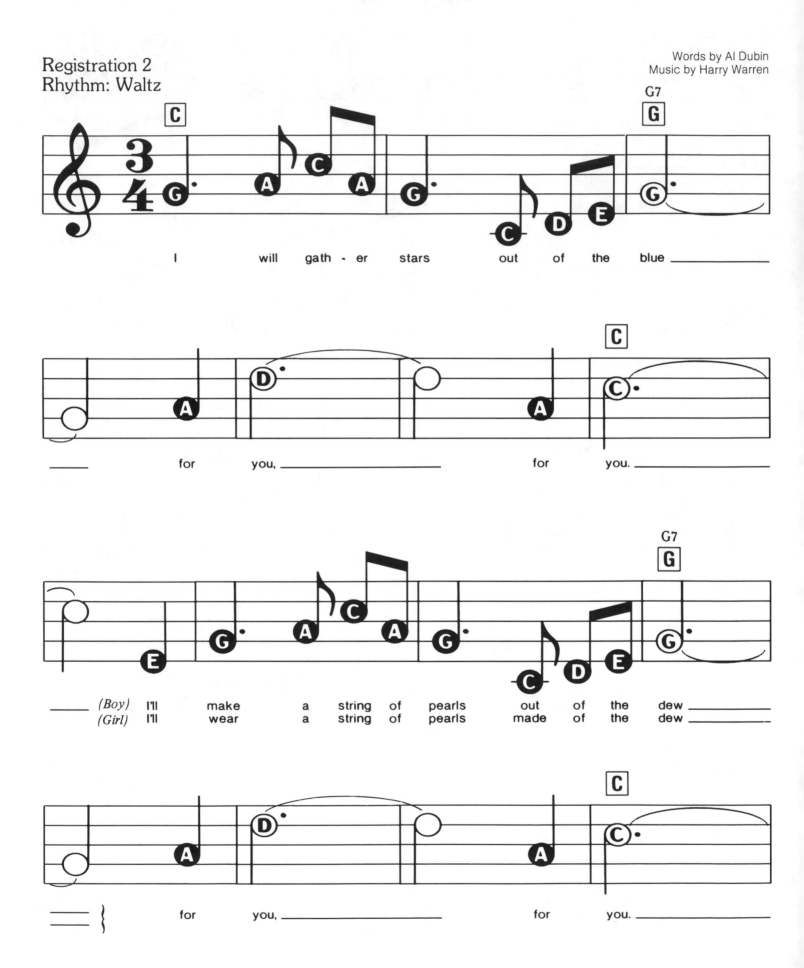

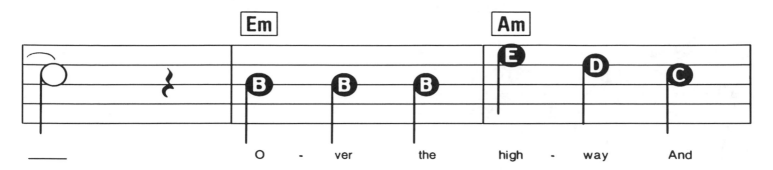

O - ver the high - way And

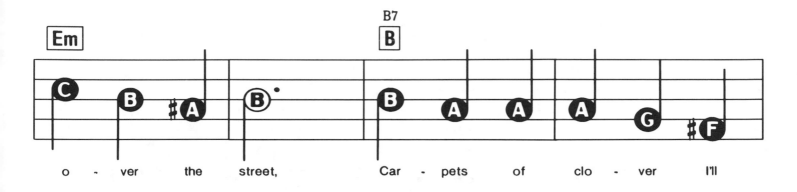

o - ver the street, Car - pets of clo - ver I'll

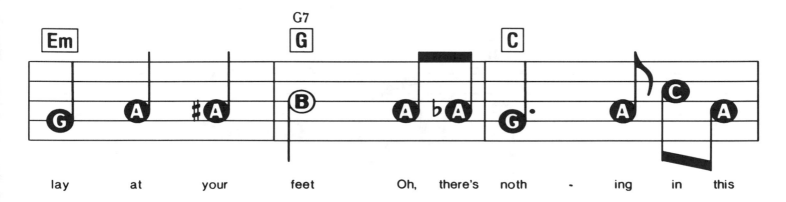

lay at your feet Oh, there's noth - ing in this

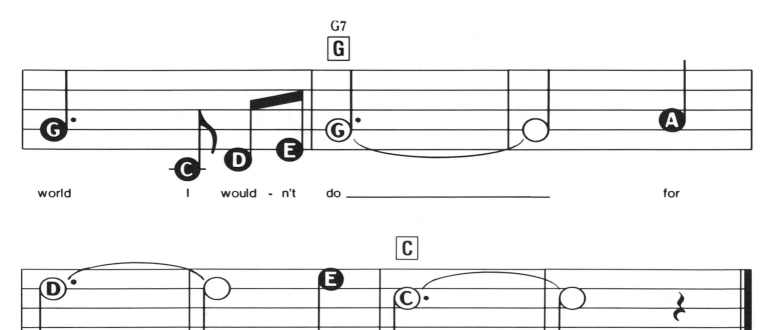

world I would - n't do _____ for

you, _____ for you. _____

Go Away, Little Girl

Registration 3
Rhythm: Slow Rock or Ballad

Words and Music by
Gerry Goffin and Carole King

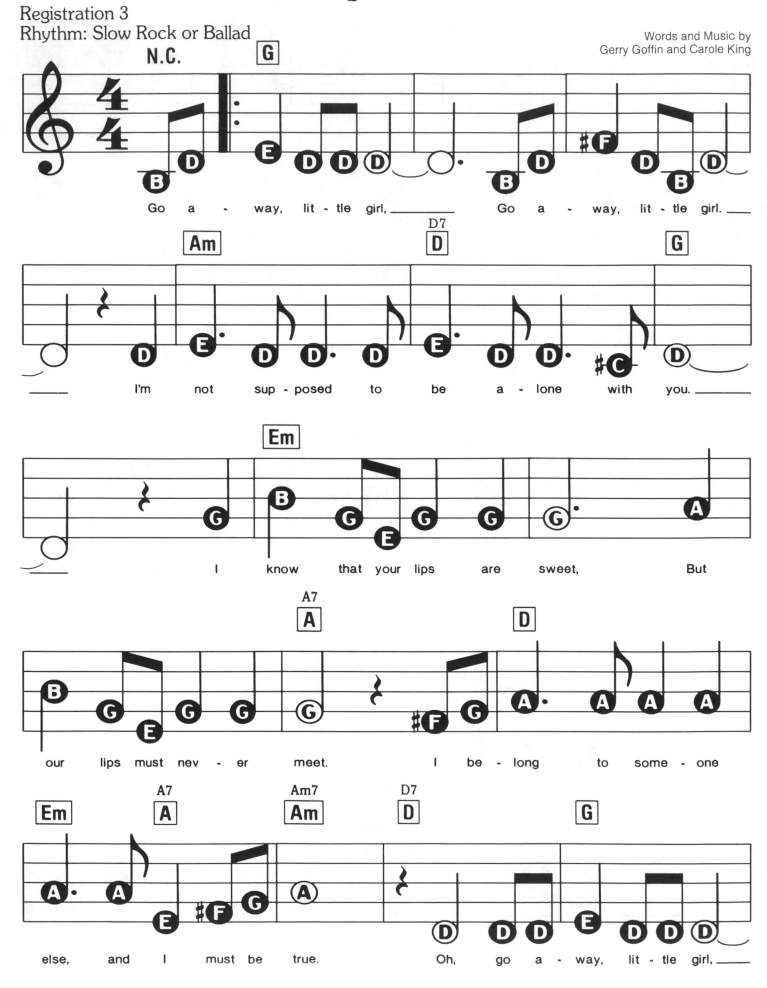

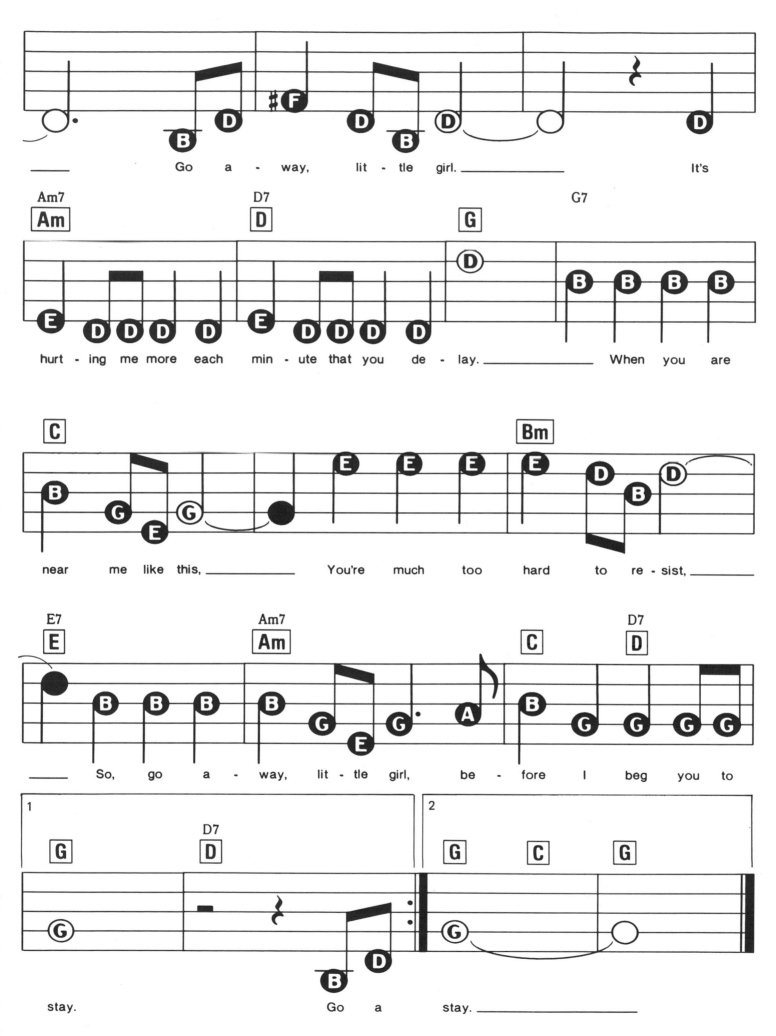

The Gold Diggers' Song
(We're In The Money)

Registration 4
Rhythm: March or Polka

Words by Al Dubin
Music by Harry Warren

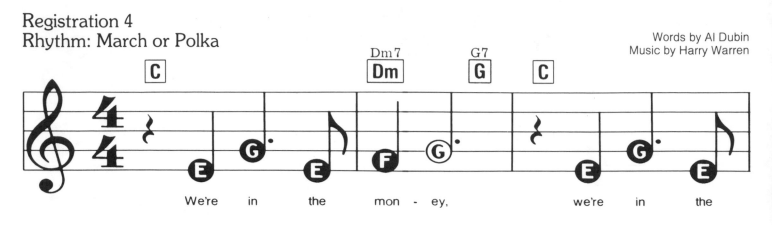

We're in the mon - ey,   we're in the

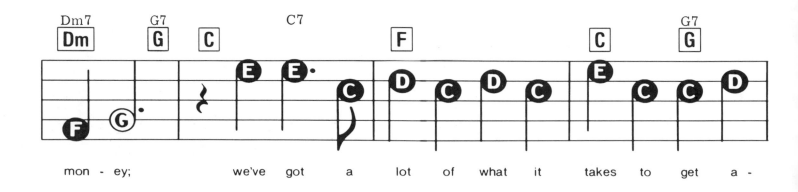

mon - ey;   we've got a lot of what it takes to get a -

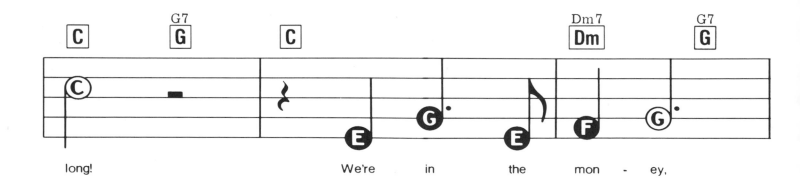

long!   We're in the mon - ey,

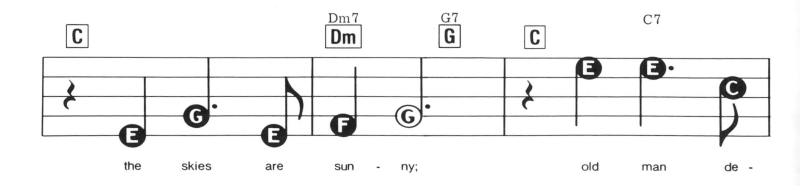

the skies are sun - ny;   old man de -

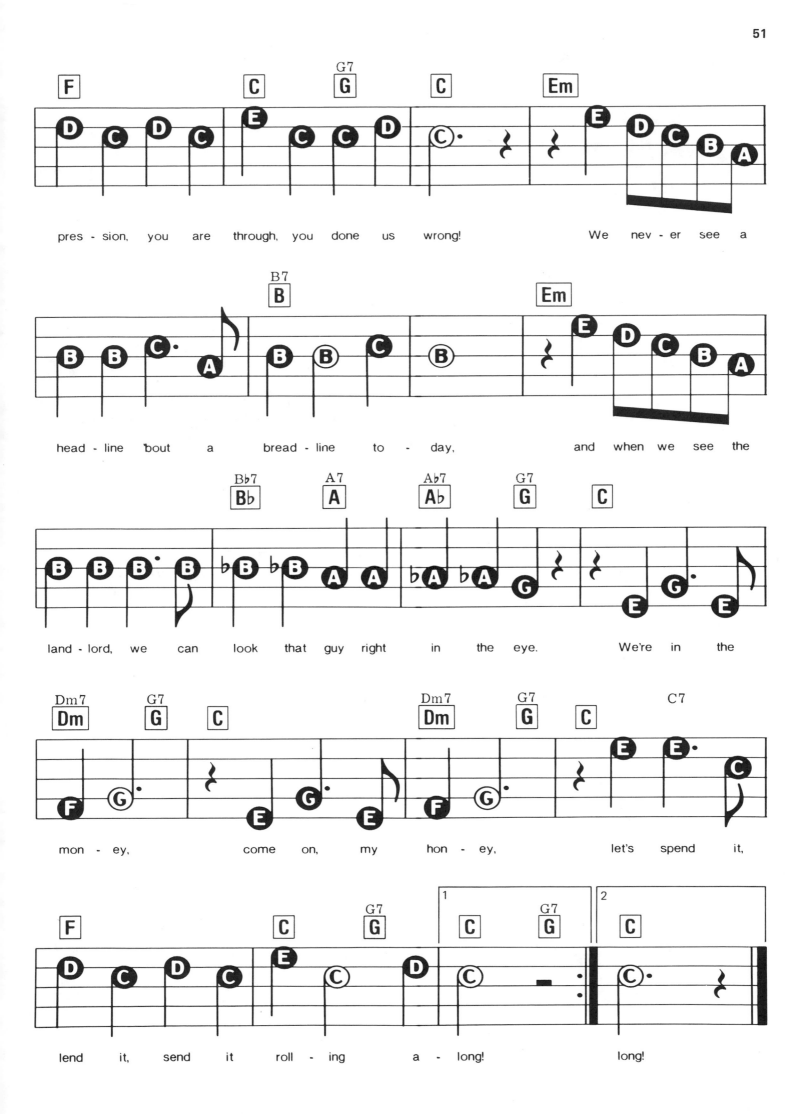

Goody, Goody

Registration 5
Rhythm: Fox Trot or Swing

Words and Music by
Johnny Mercer and Matt Malneck

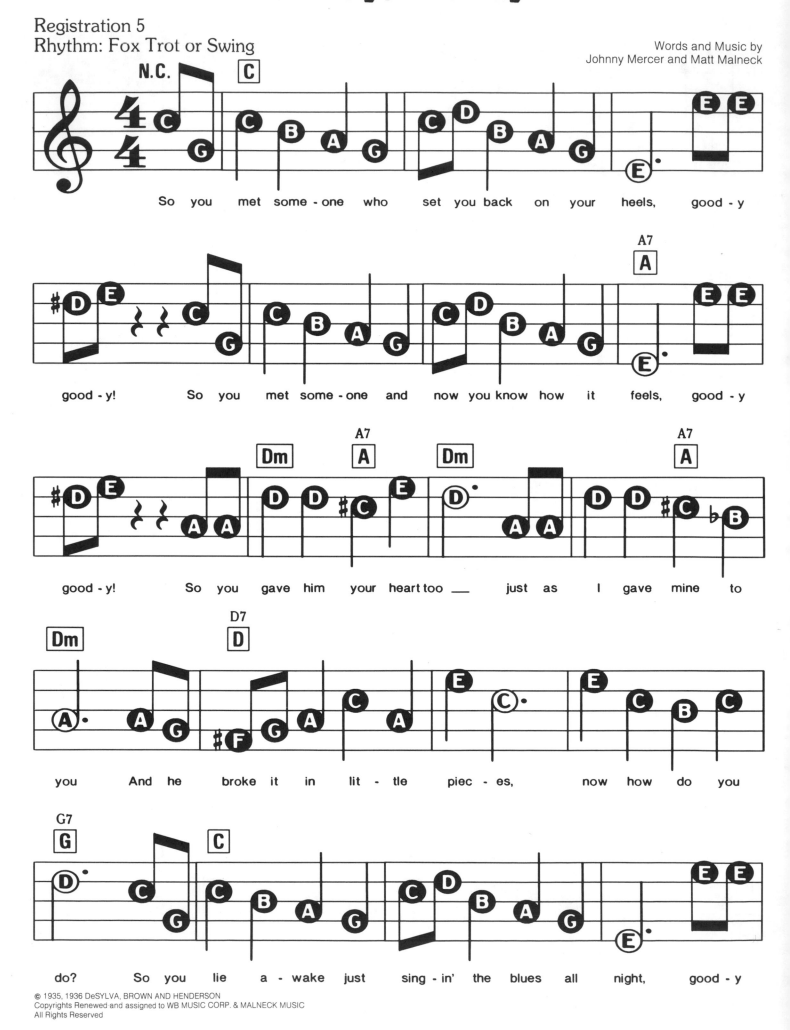

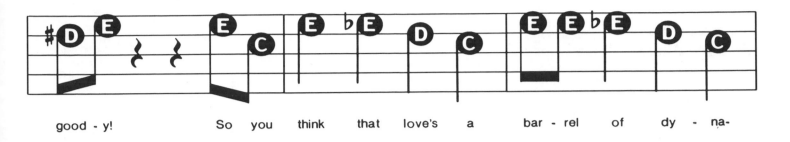

C7

good - y! So you think that love's a bar - rel of dy - na-

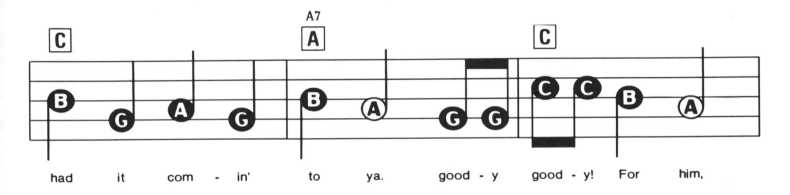

F   Fm

mite. _____ Hoo - ray and hal - le - lu - jah! You

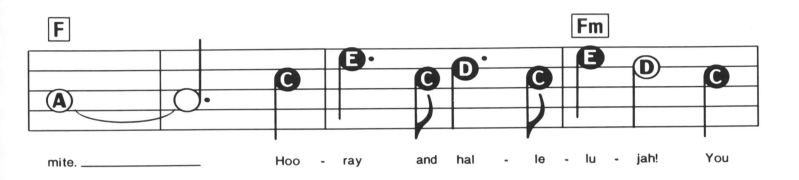

C   A7   C
                     A

had it com - in' to ya. good - y good - y! For him,

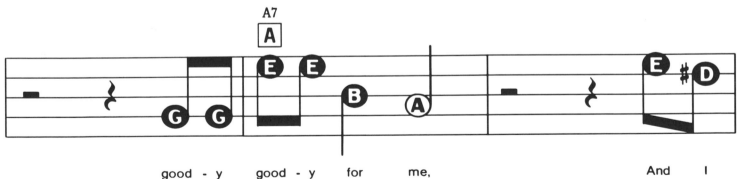

A7
A

good - y good - y for me,   And I

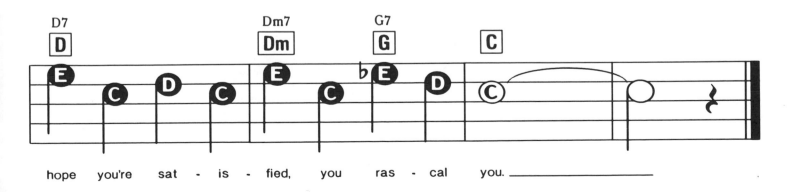

D7   Dm7   G7
D   Dm   G   C

hope you're sat - is - fied, you ras - cal you. _____

He'll Have To Go

Registration 5
Rhythm: Waltz

Words and Music by
Joe Allison and Audrey Allison

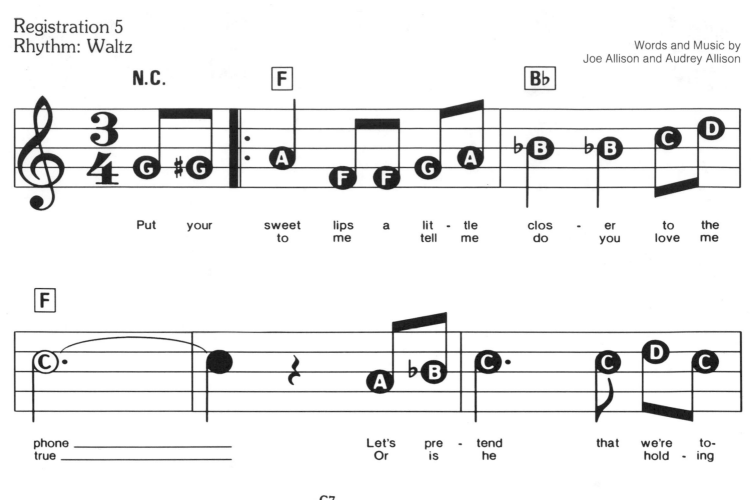

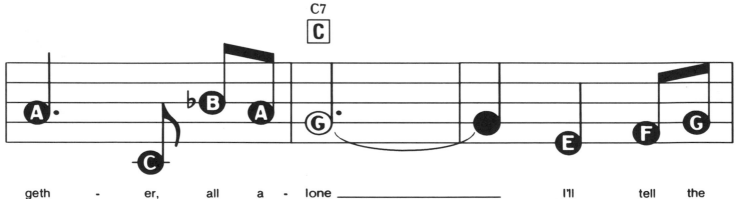

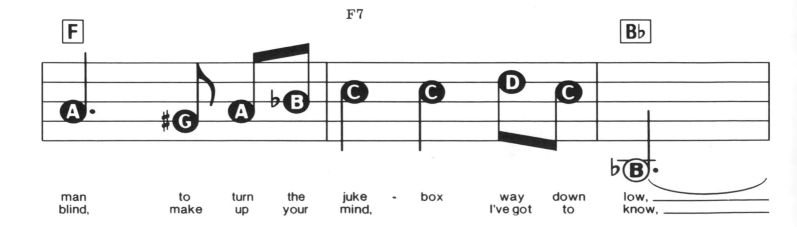

And you can tell your friend, there with you, He'll have to
Should I

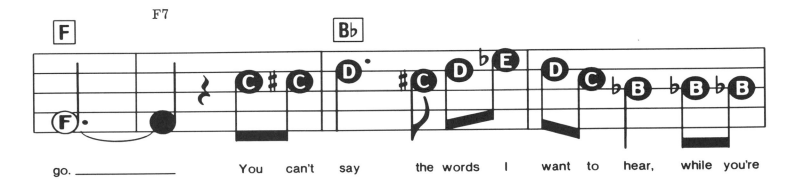

go. Whis - per hang up or will you tell him he'll have to

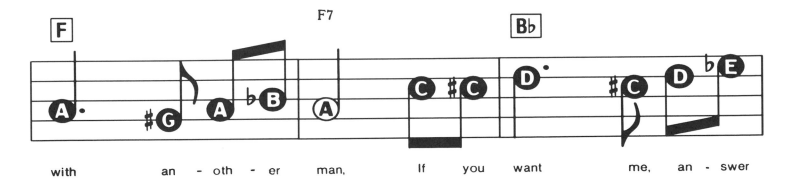

go. _____ You can't say the words I want to hear, while you're

with an - oth - er man, If you want me, an - swer

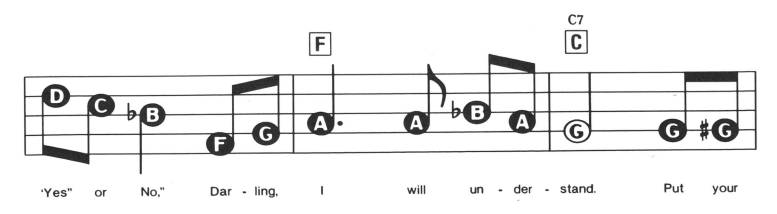

'Yes" or No," Dar - ling, I will un - der - stand. Put your

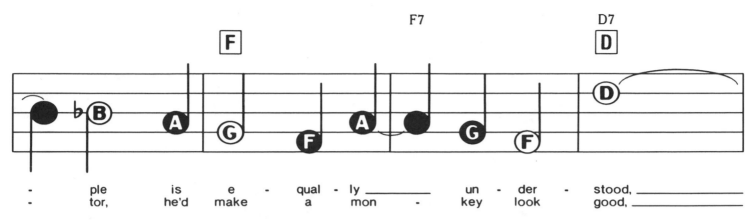

59

- ple   is   e - qual - ly _____ un - der - stood, _____
- tor,   he'd   make   a   mon - key   look   good, _____

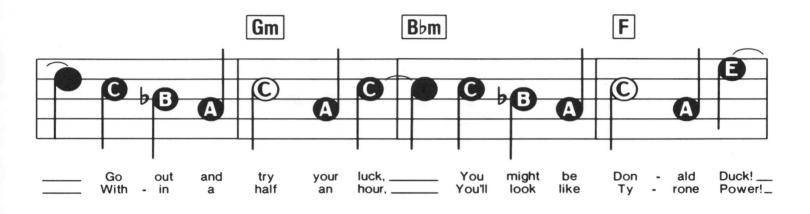

_____ Go   out and try your luck, _____ You might be Don - ald Duck! __
_____ With - in a half an hour, _____ You'll look like Ty - rone Power! __

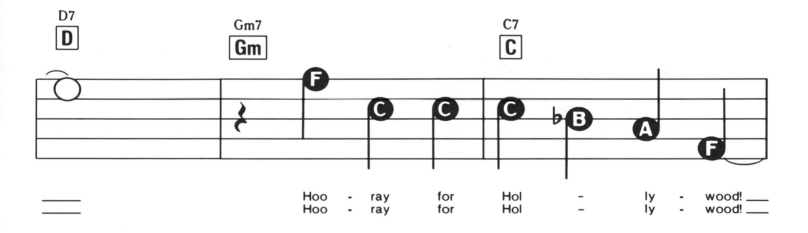

_____   Hoo - ray for Hol - ly - wood! __
                   Hoo - ray for Hol - ly - wood! __

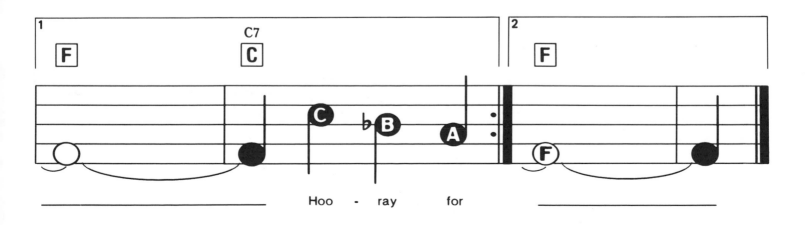

_____   Hoo - ray for _____

I Believe In Music

Registration 10
Rhythm: Rock

Words and Music by
Mac Davis

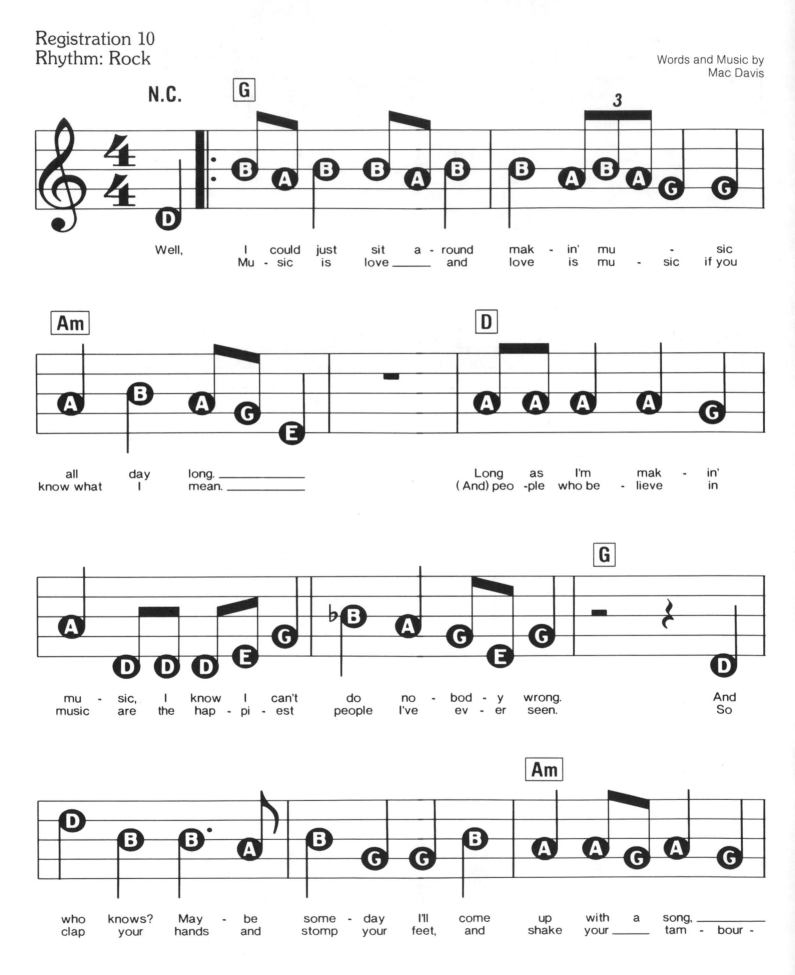

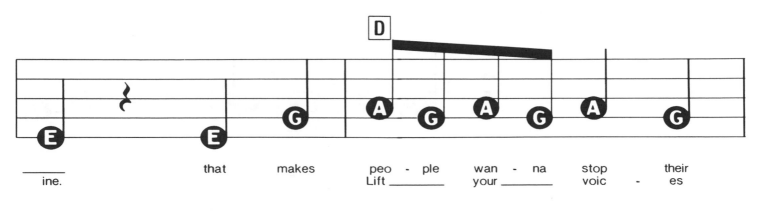

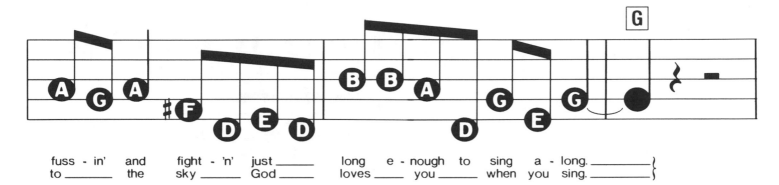

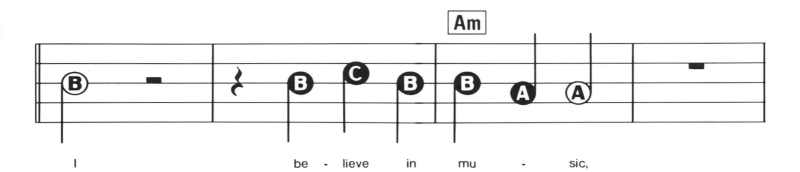

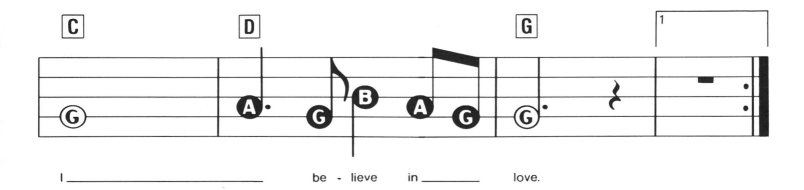

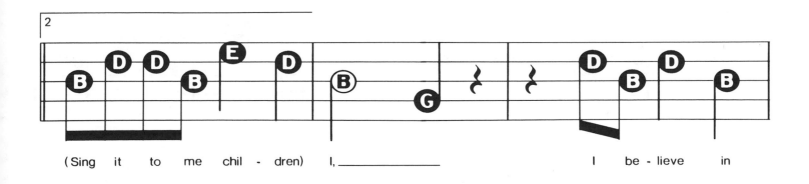

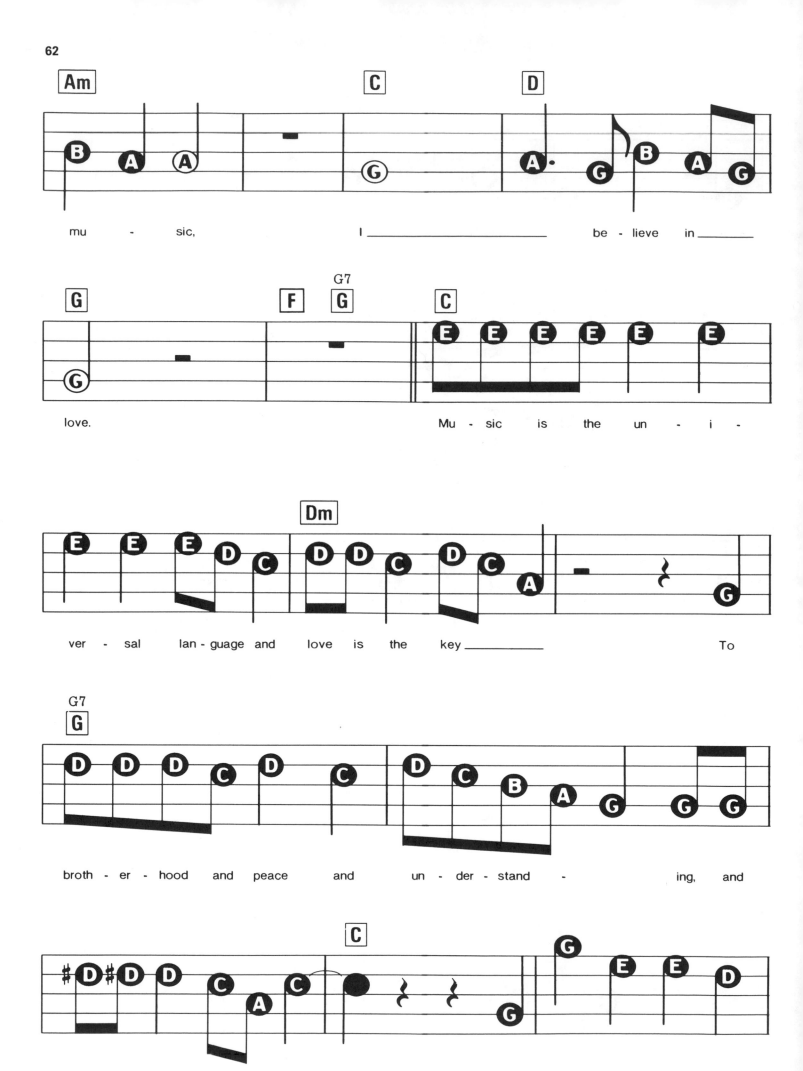

63

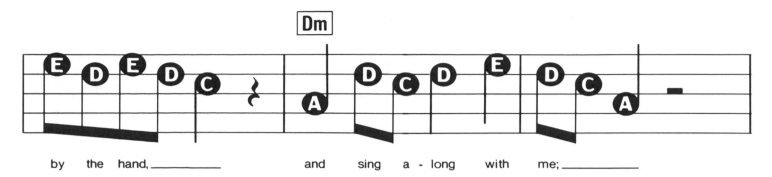

by the hand,_____ and sing a - long with me;_____

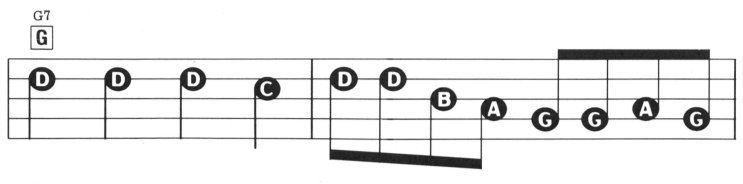

find out what it real - ly means_____ to feel_____

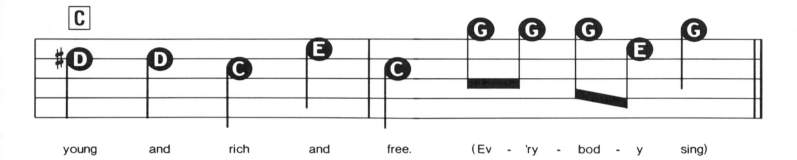

young and rich and free. (Ev - 'ry - bod - y sing)

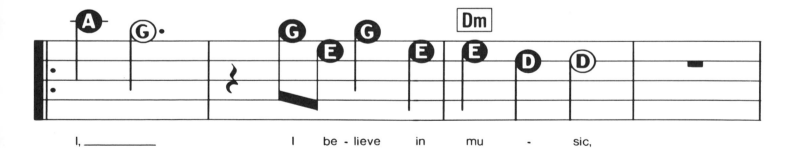

I,_____ I be - lieve in mu - sic,

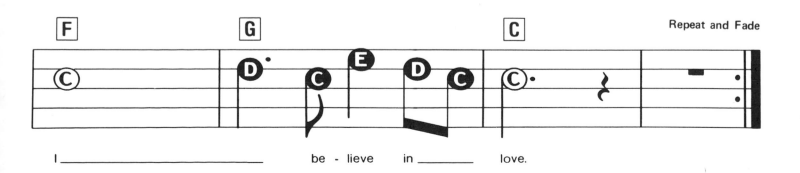

I_____ be - lieve in _____ love.

I Kiss Your Hand, Madame

Registration 9
Rhythm: Fox Trot or Swing

Original Text by Fritz Rotter
English Text by Sam Lewis & Joe Young
French Version by Emelia Renaud
Music by Ralph Erwin

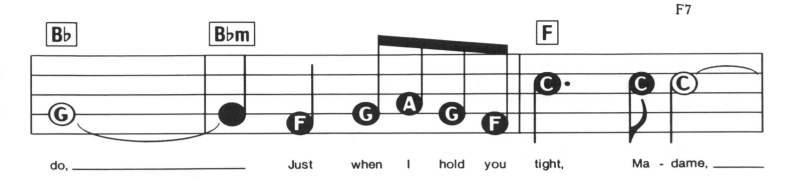

do, _____ Just when I hold you tight, Ma - dame, _____

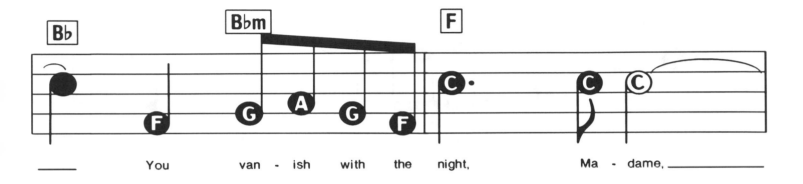

_____ You van - ish with the night, Ma - dame, _____

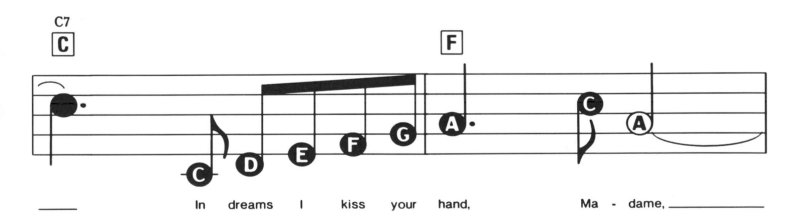

_____ In dreams I kiss your hand, Ma - dame, _____

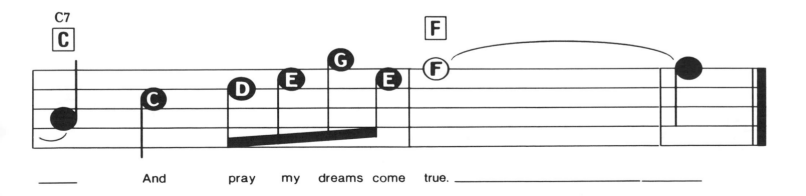

_____ And pray my dreams come true. _____

I Only Have Eyes For You

Registration 3
Rhythm: Fox Trot or Swing

Words by Al Dubin
Music by Harry Warren

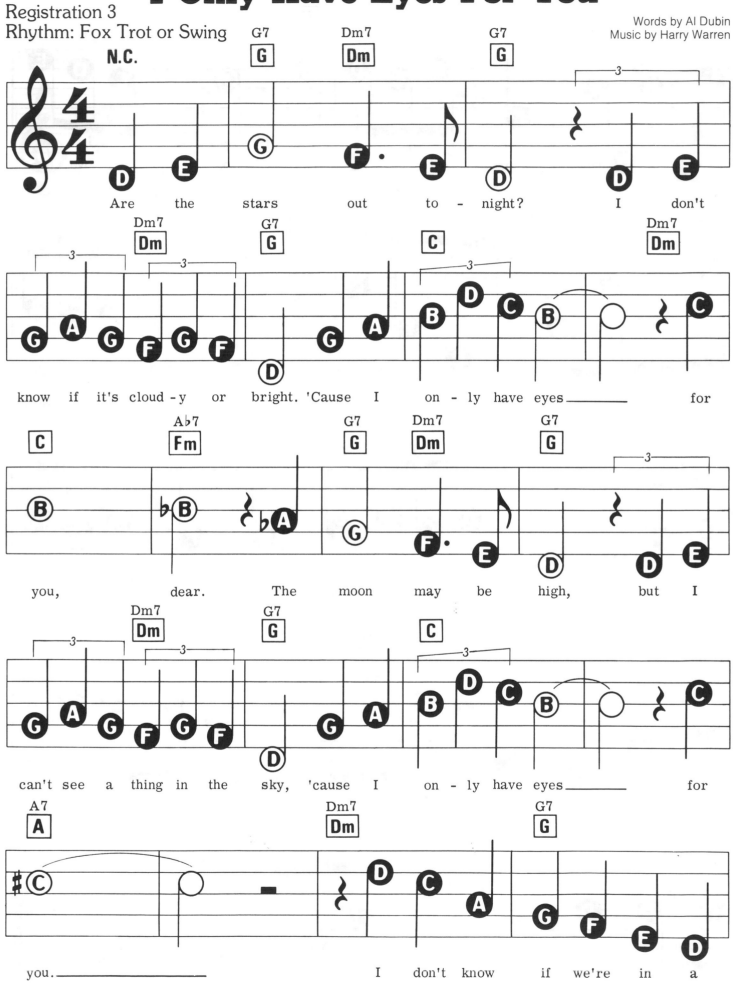

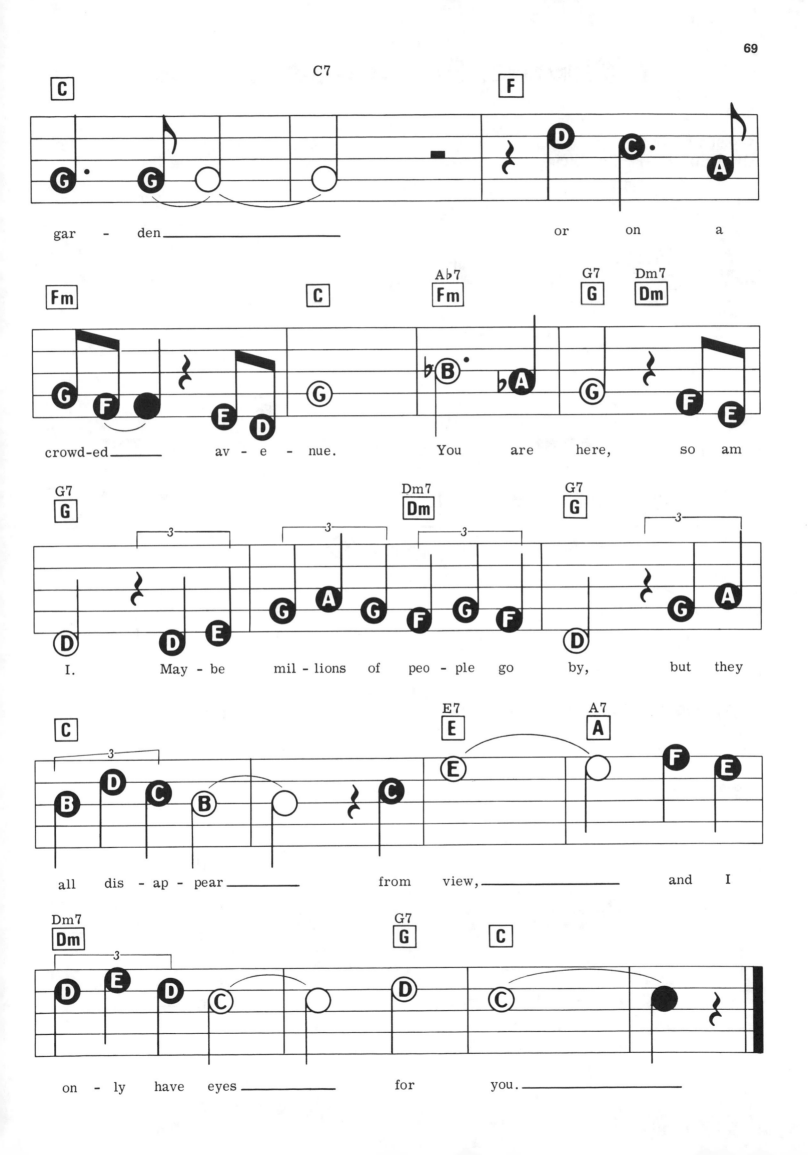

I Wanna Be Loved By You

Registration 4
Rhythm: Fox Trot or Swing

Words by Bert Kalmar
Music by Herbert Stothart & Harry Ruby

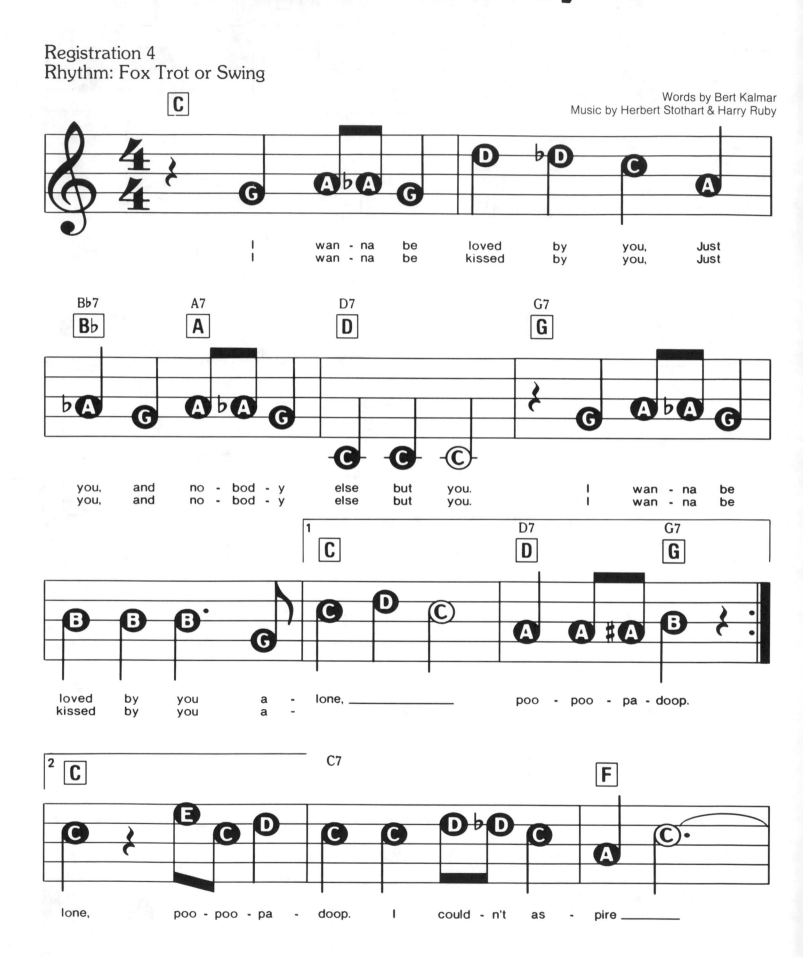

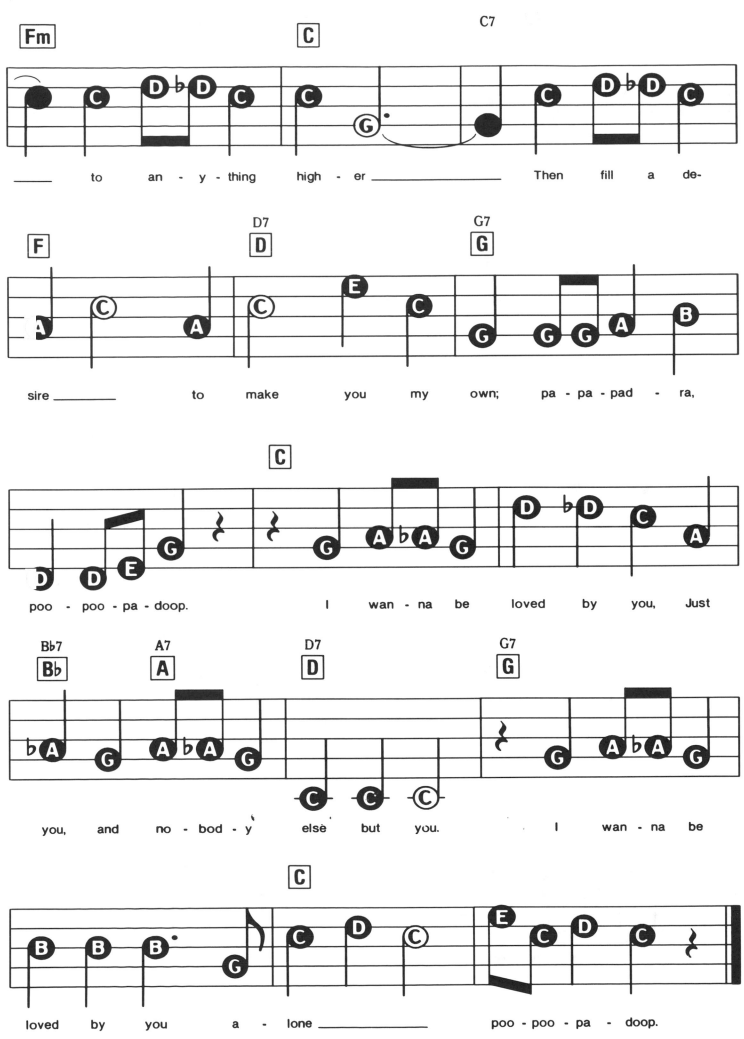

74

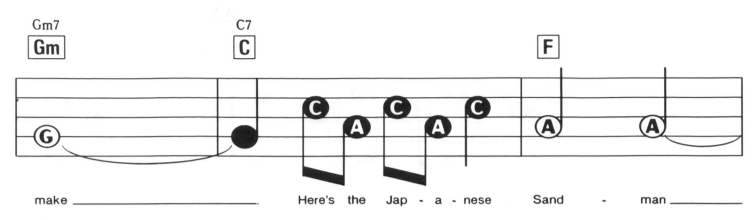

make _____ Here's the Jap - a - nese Sand - man _____

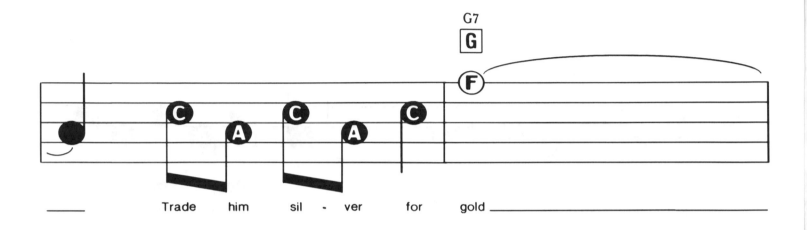

_____ Trade him sil - ver for gold _____

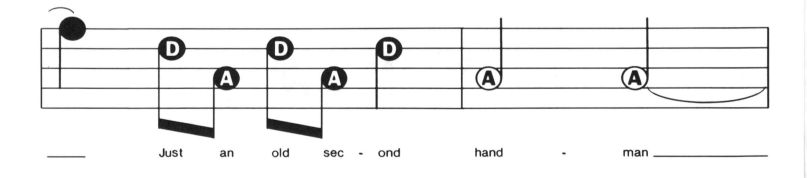

_____ Just an old sec - ond hand - man _____

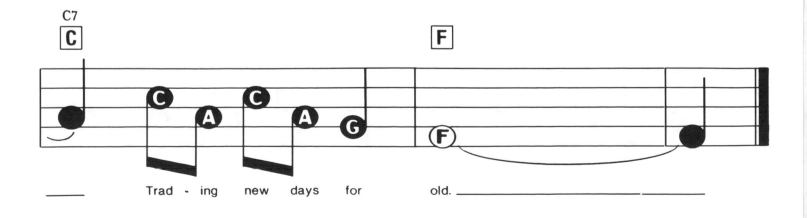

_____ Trad - ing new days for old. _____

On The Boardwalk
(In Atlantic City)
(From the Twentieth Century-Fox Musical "THREE LITTLE GIRLS IN BLUE")

Registration 4
Rhythm: Waltz

Lyric by Mack Gordon
Music by Josef Myrow

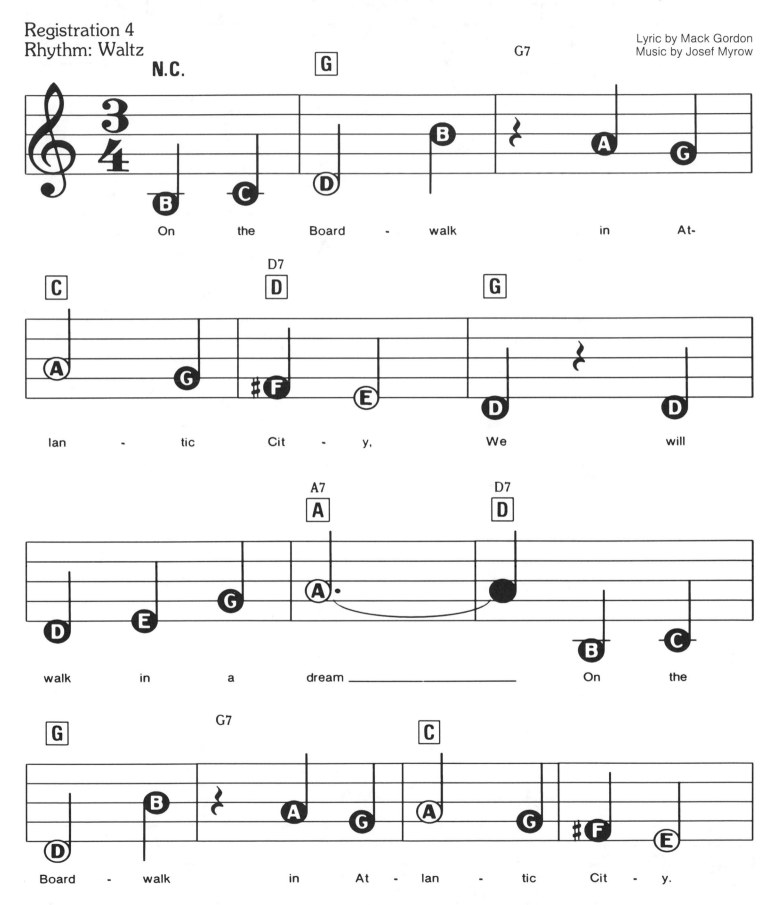

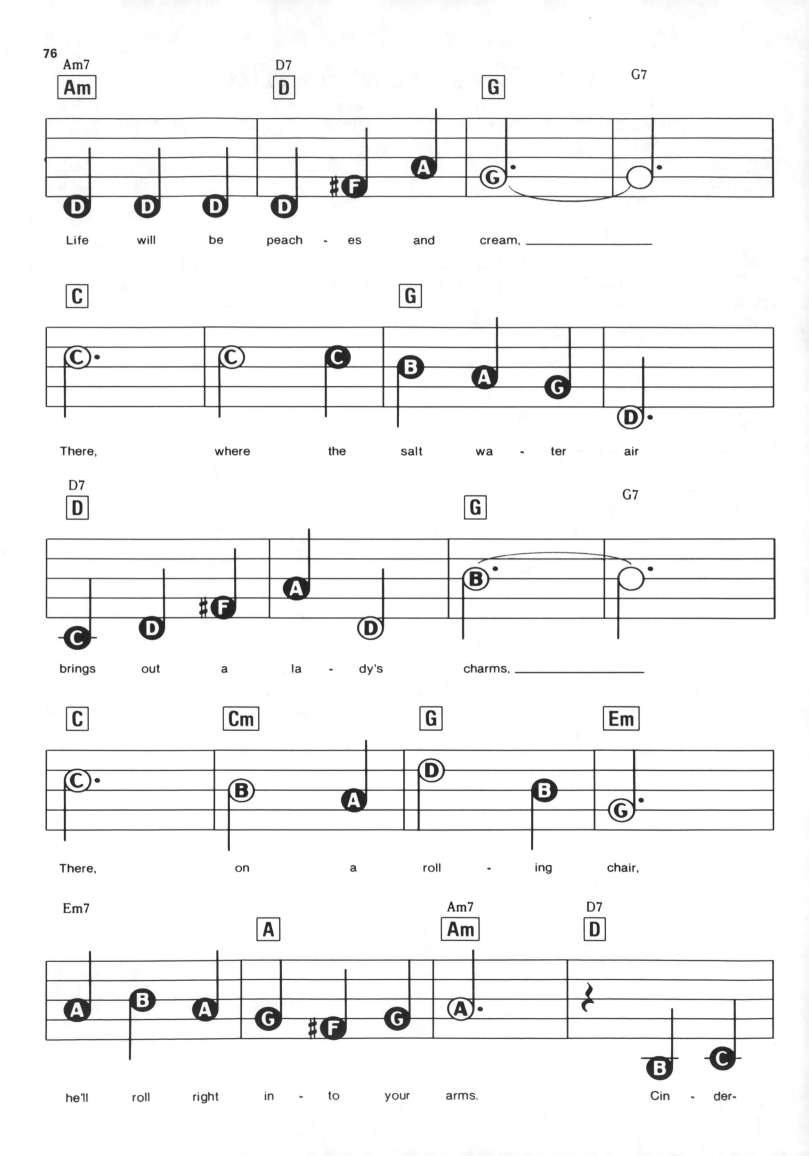

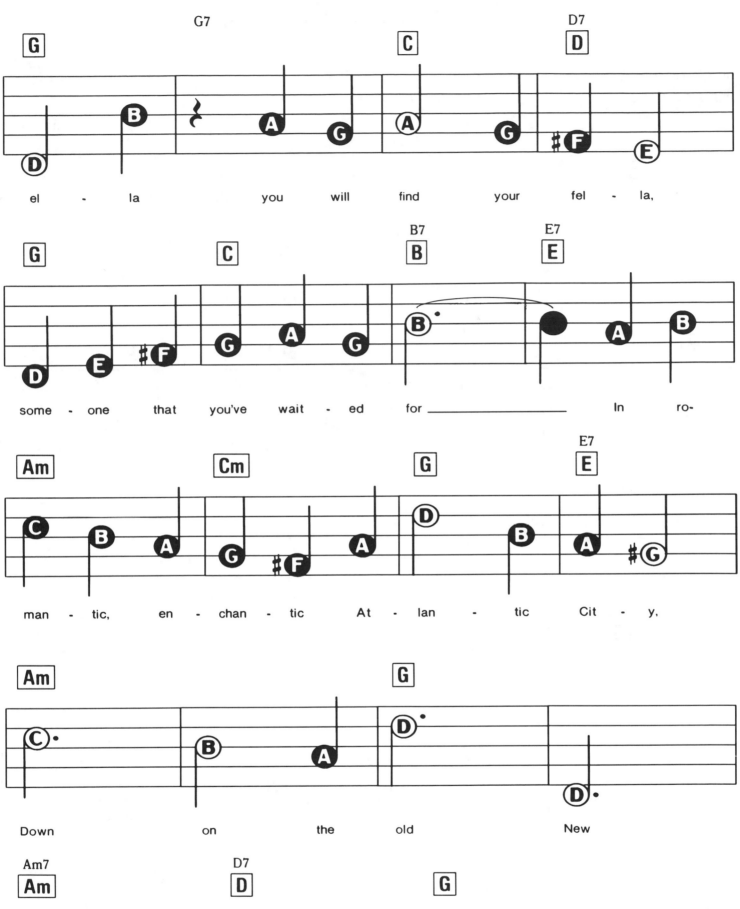

el - la   you will find your fel - la,

some - one that you've wait - ed for _____ In ro-

man - tic, en - chan - tic At - lan - tic Cit - y,

Down   on   the   old   New

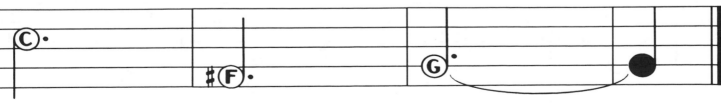

Jer - sey   Shore. _____

Kiss Me Again

Registration 3
Rhythm: Waltz

Words by Henry Blossom
Music by Victor Herbert

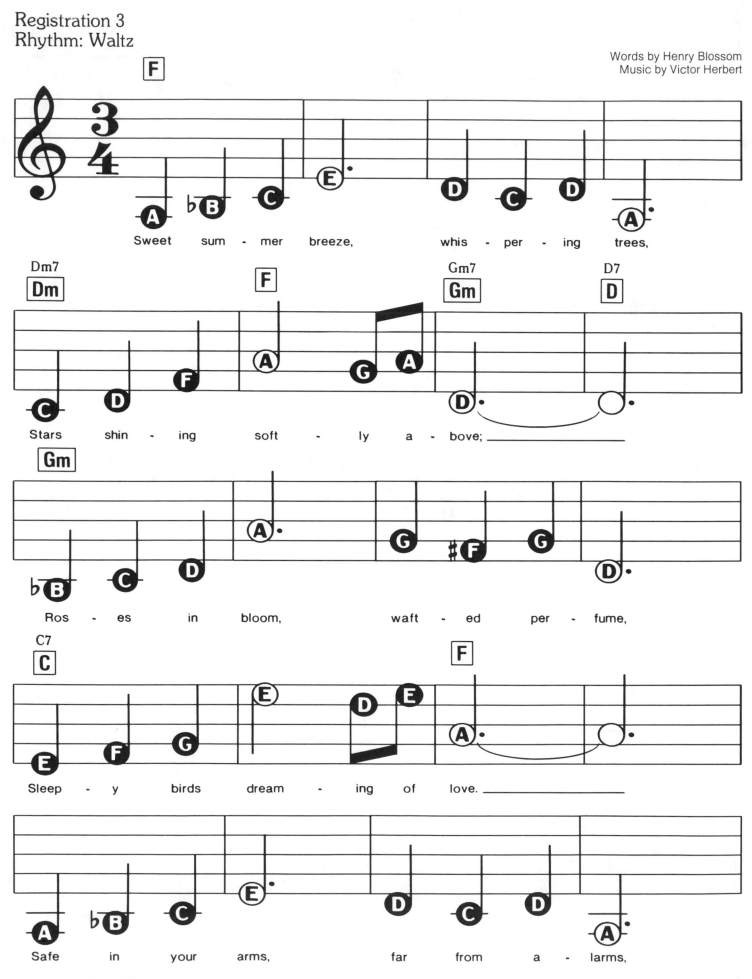

L'Amour Toujours, L'Amour

(Love Everlasting)

Registration 5
Rhythm: Waltz

Words by Catherine Chisholm Cushing
Music by Rudolf Friml

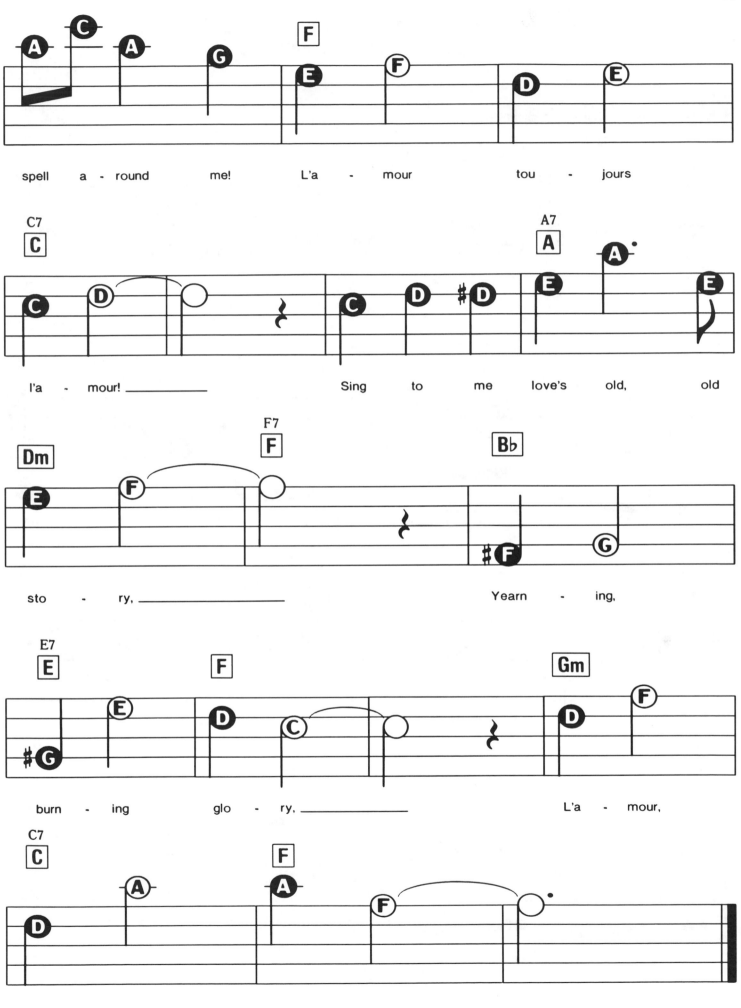

A Little Bit Of Heaven
(Shure They Call It Ireland)

Registration 9
Rhythm: Slow Rock or Ballad

Words by J. Keirn Brenan
Music by Ernest R. Ball

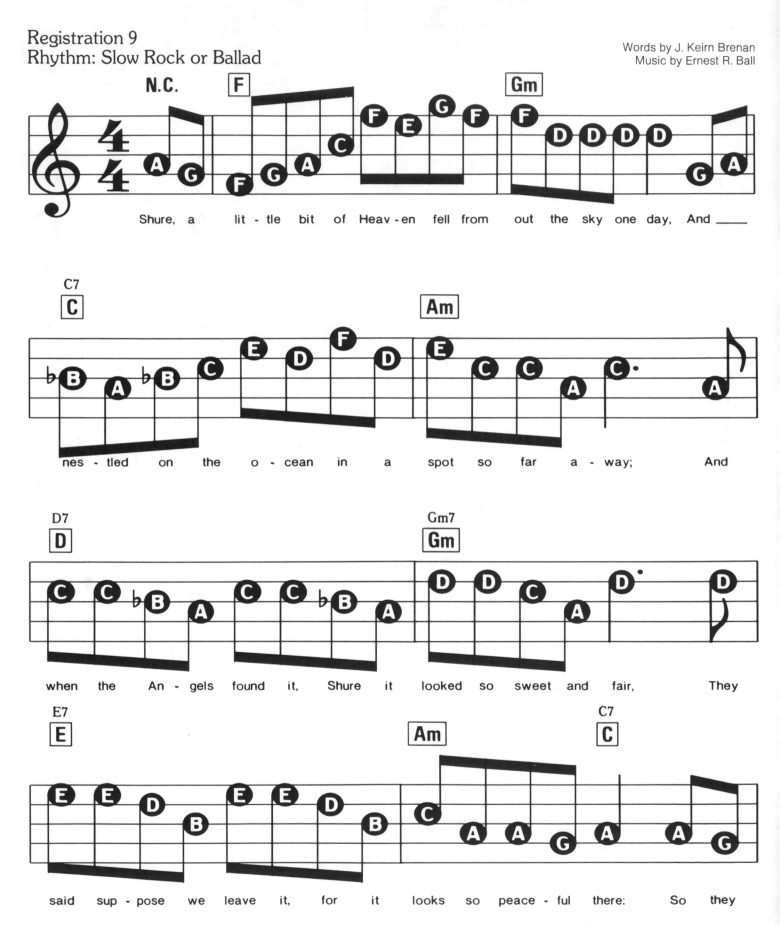

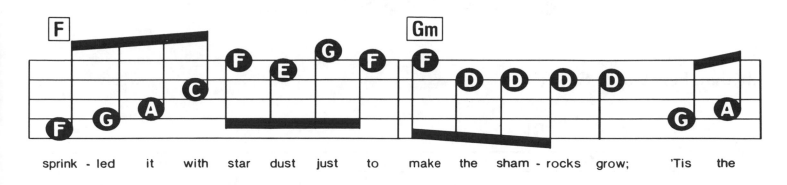

sprink - led it with star dust just to make the sham - rocks grow; 'Tis the

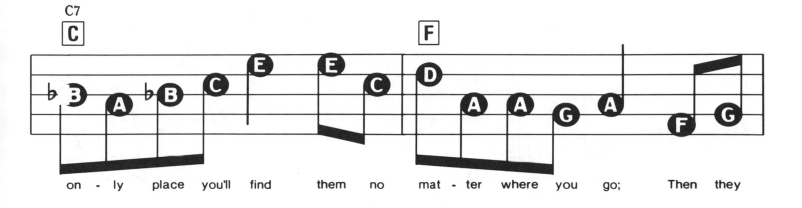

on - ly place you'll find them no mat - ter where you go; Then they

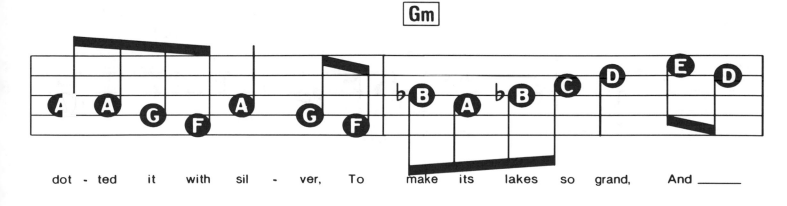

dot - ted it with sil - ver, To make its lakes so grand, And ____ the

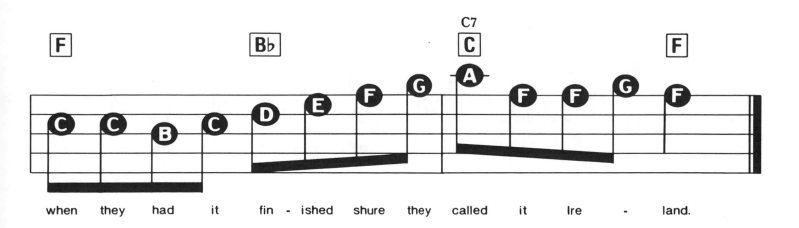

when they had it fin - ished shure they called it Ire - land.

Little White Lies

Registration 2
Rhythm: Fox Trot or Swing

Words and Music by
Walter Donaldson

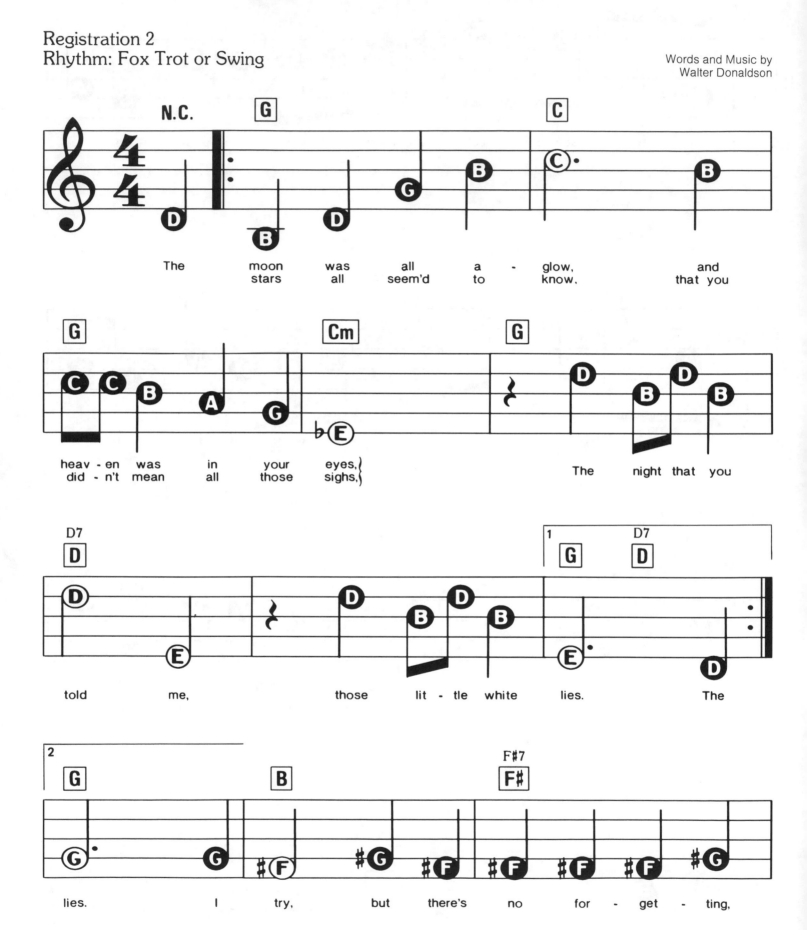

85

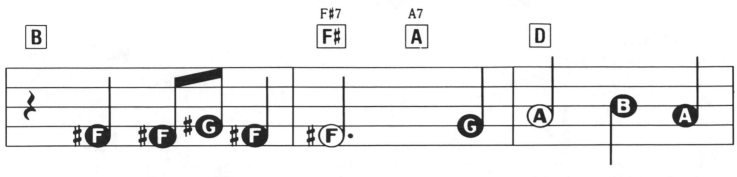

when eve - ning ap - pears. I sigh, but there's

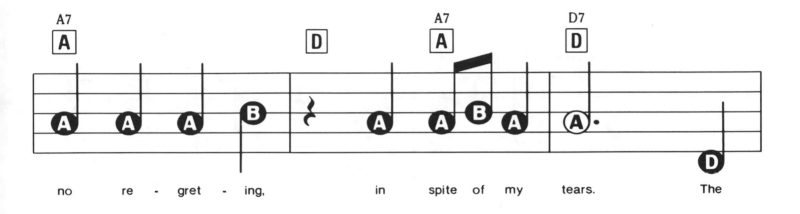

no re - gret - ing, in spite of my tears. The

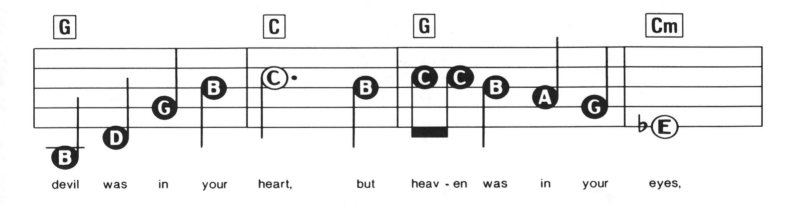

devil was in your heart, but heav - en was in your eyes,

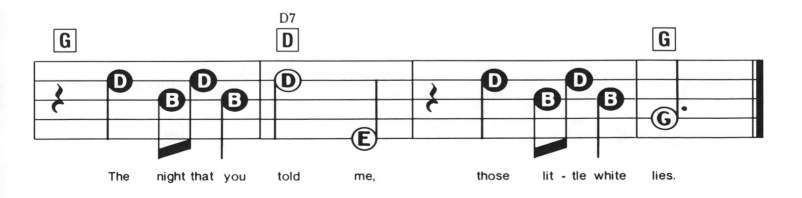

The night that you told me, those lit - tle white lies.

The Look Of Love

Registration 4
Rhythm: Bossa Nova

Words by Hal David
Music by Burt Bacharach

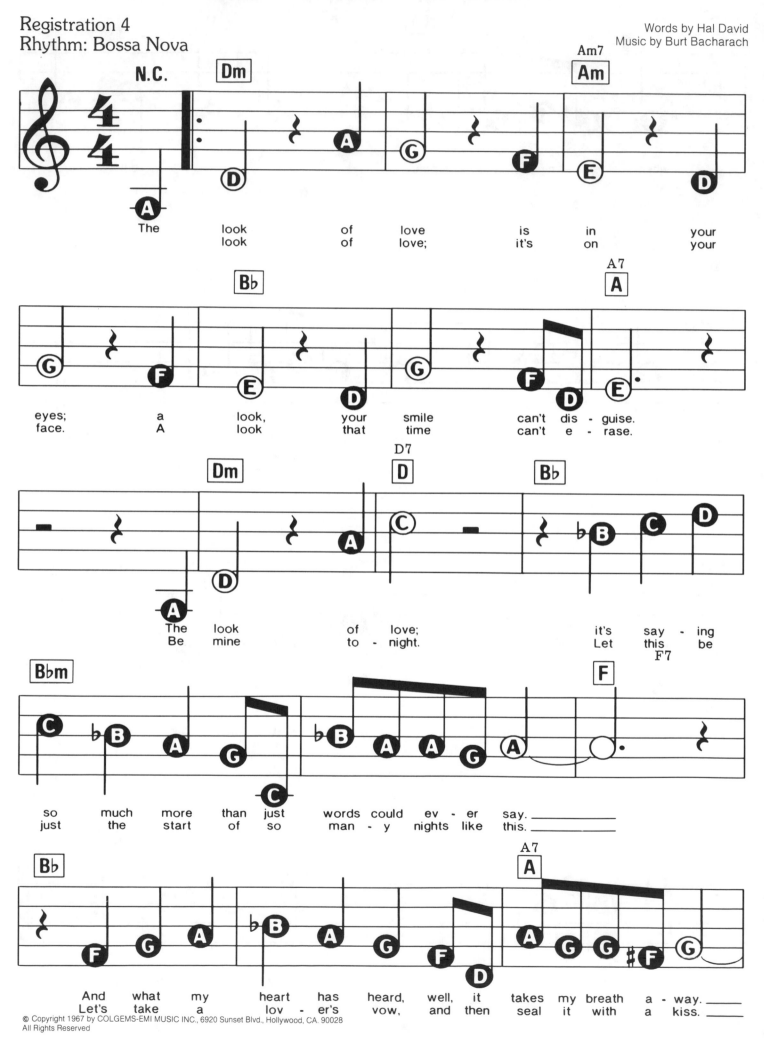

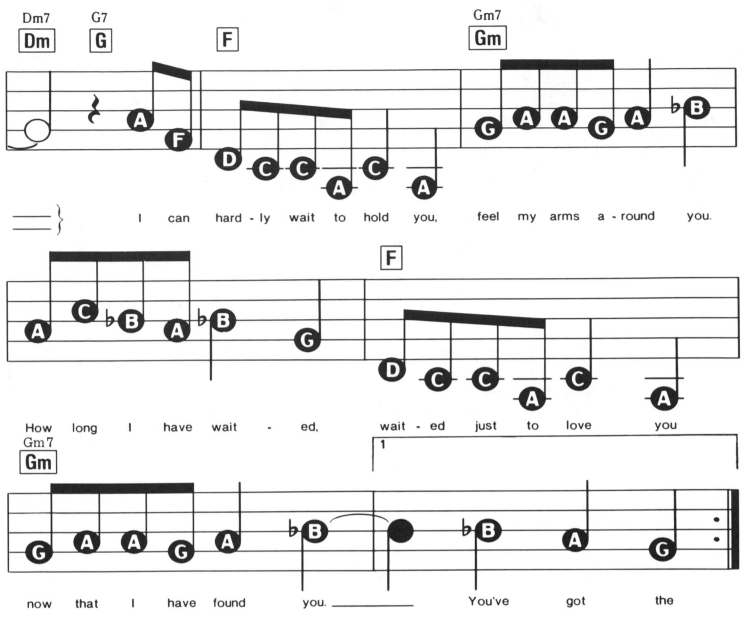

I can hard-ly wait to hold you, feel my arms a-round you.

How long I have wait - ed, wait - ed just to love you

now that I have found you. _____ You've got the

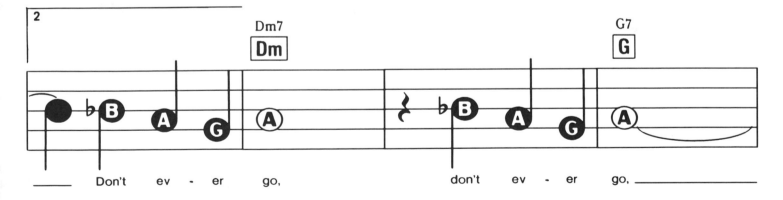

_____ Don't ev - er go, don't ev - er go, _____

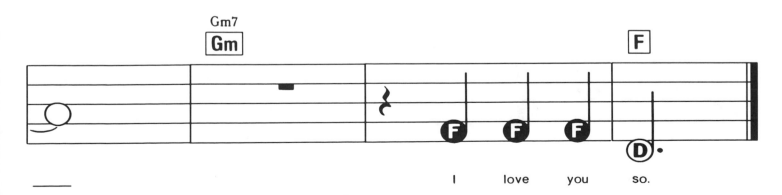

I love you so.

Love Me Or Leave Me

Words by Gus Kahn
Music by Walter Donaldson

Registration 4
Rhythm: Fox Trot or Swing

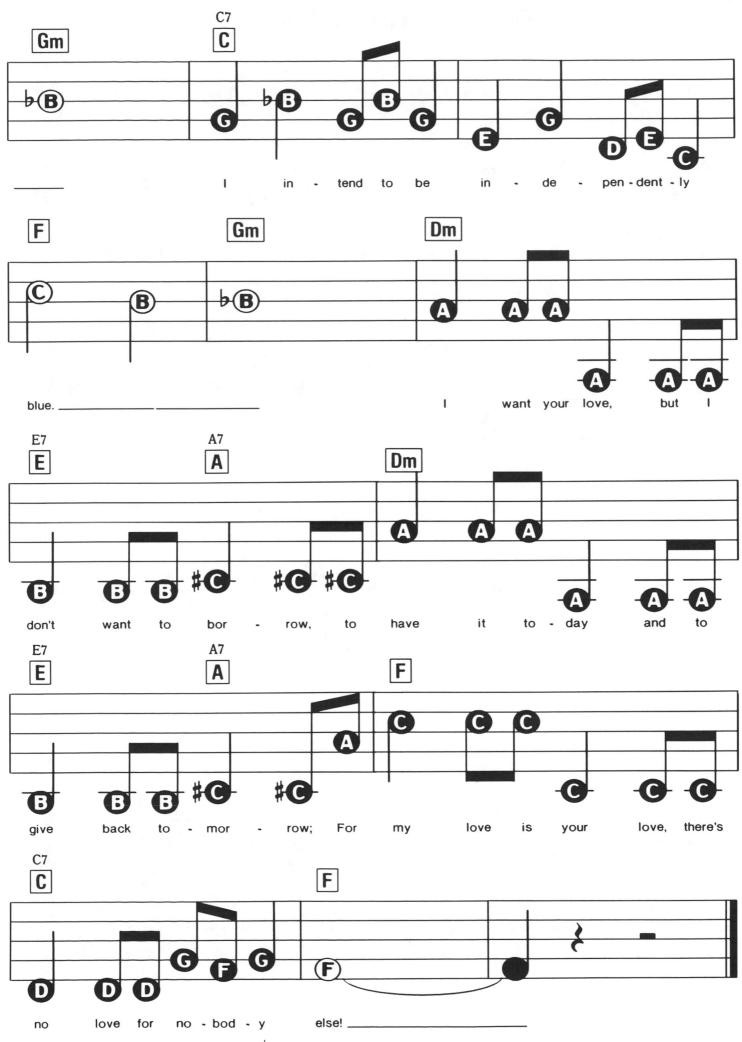

The Love Nest

Words and Music by
Louis A. Hirsch and Otto A. Harbach

Registration 9
Rhythm: Fox Trot or Swing

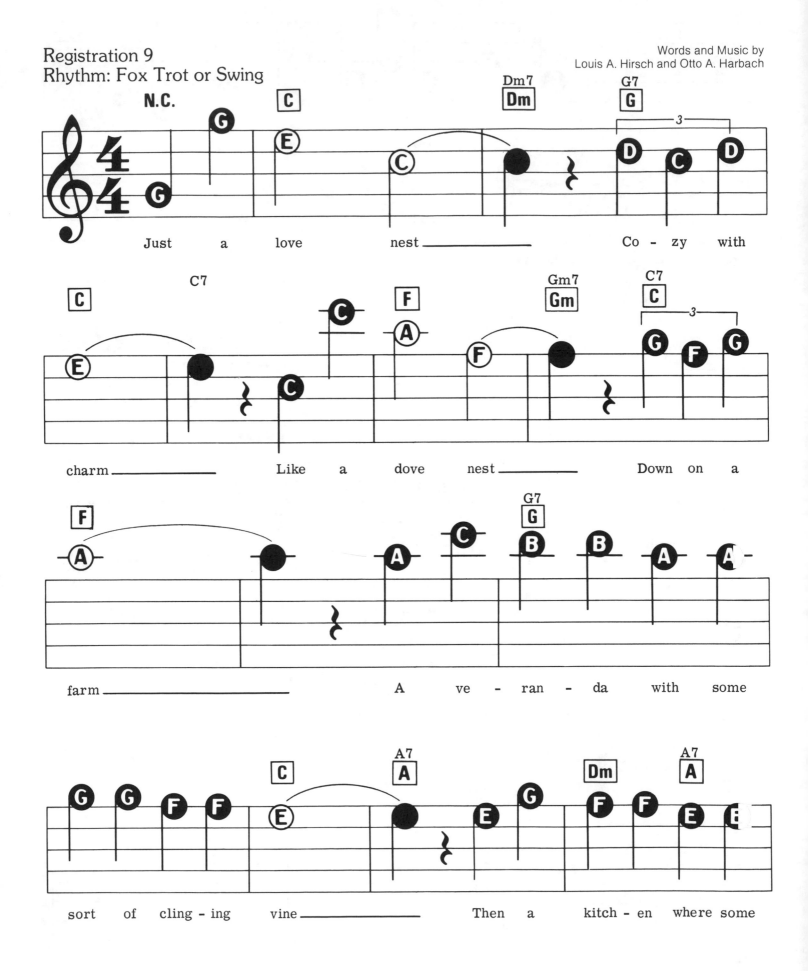

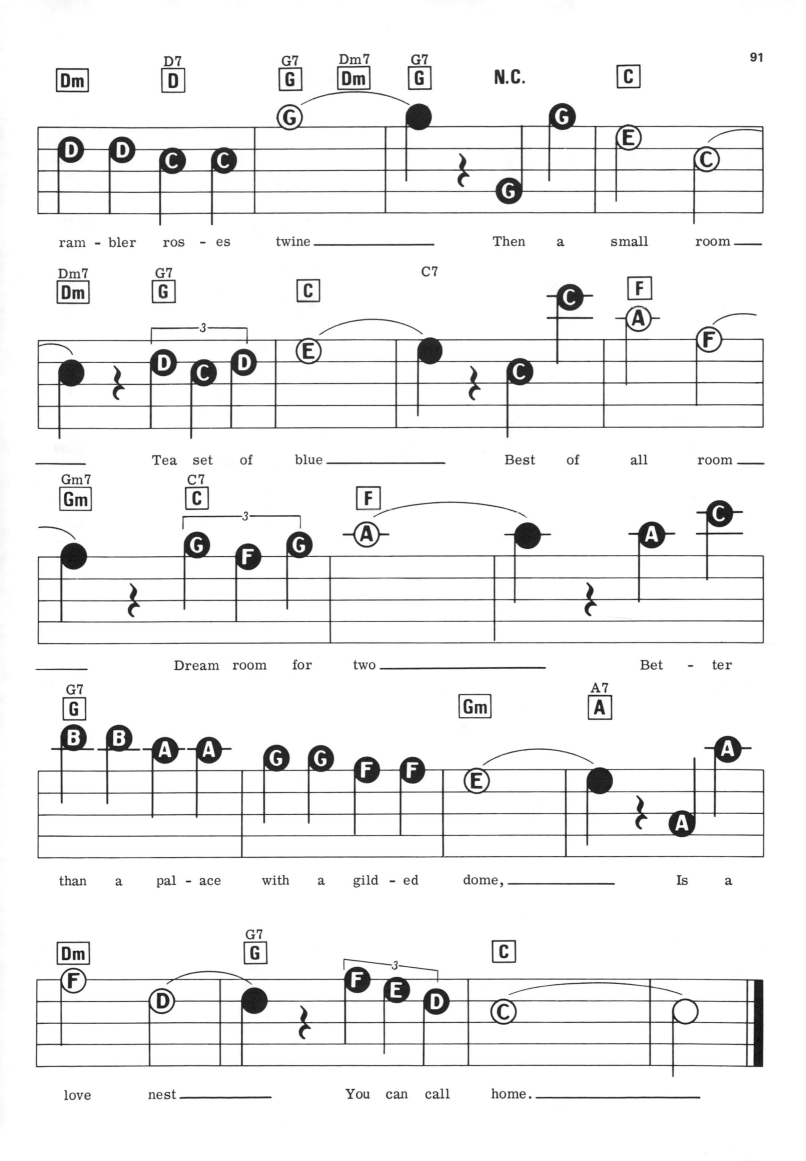

Makin' Whoopee!

Registration 5
Rhythm: Fox Trot or Swing

Words by Gus Kahn
Music by Walter Donaldson

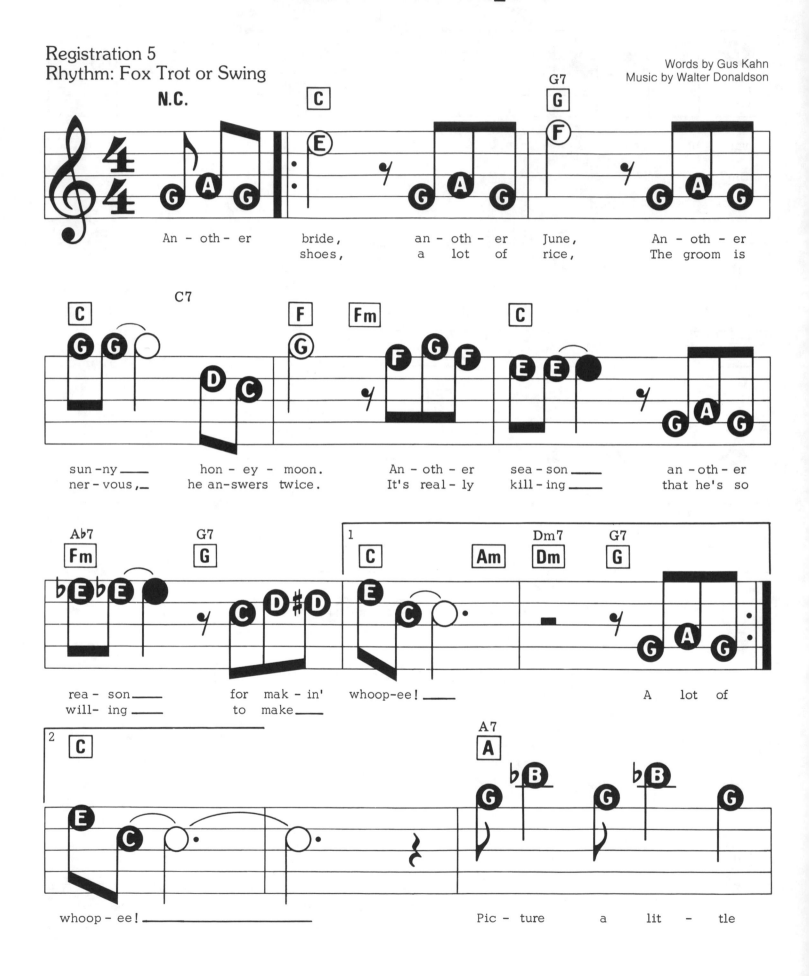

93

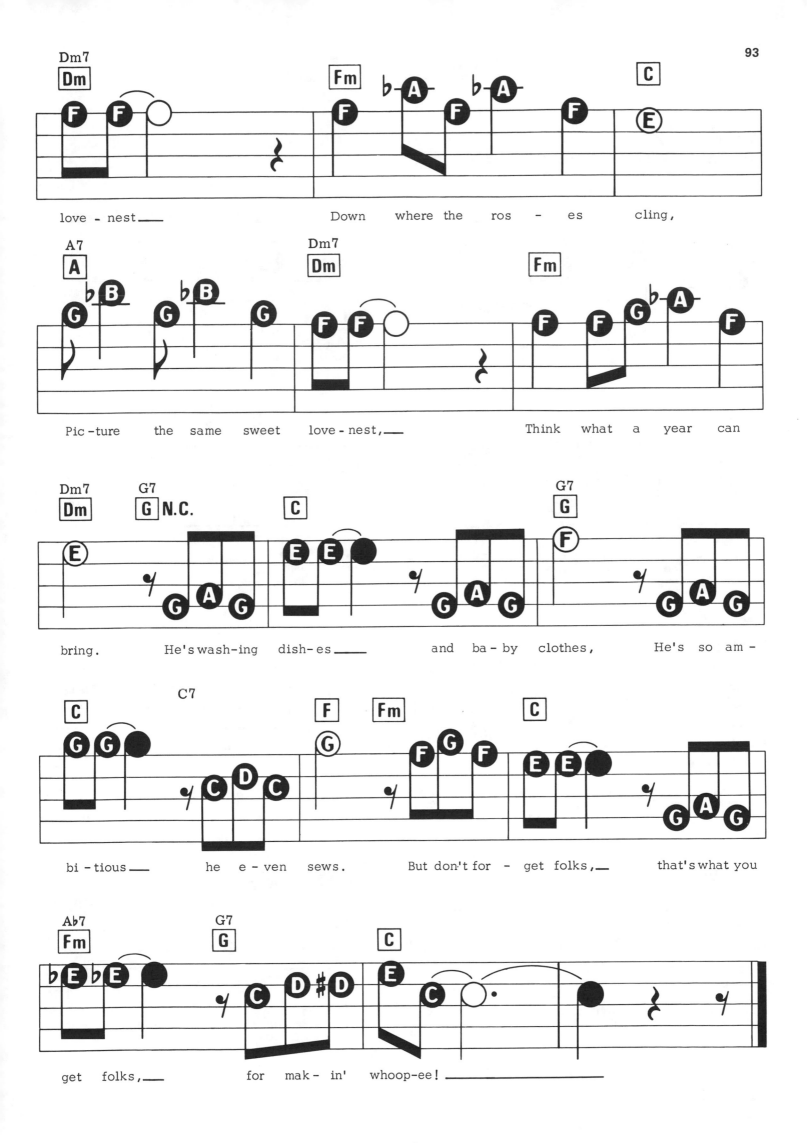

Midnight Sun

Registration 2
Rhythm: Fox Trot or Ballad

Words and Music by
John Wetton and Geoffrey Downes

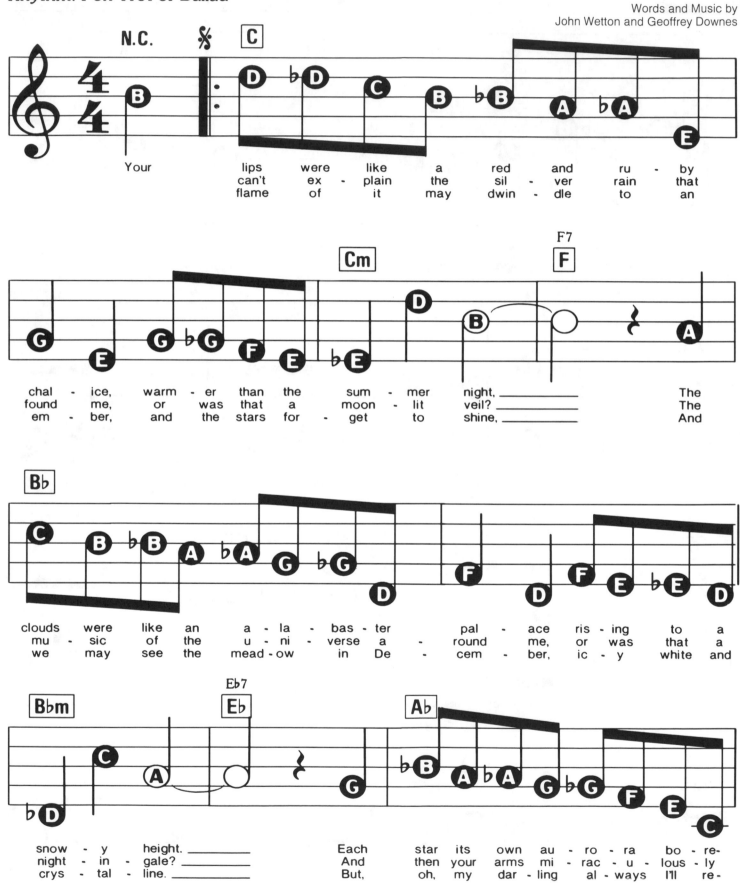

95

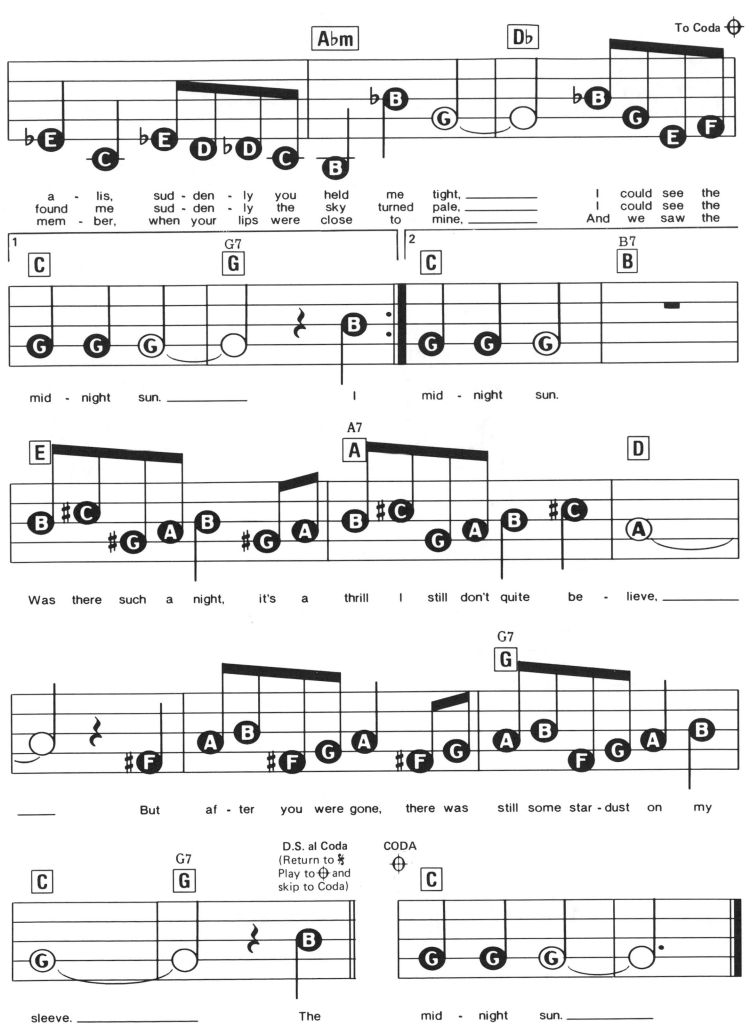

Mine
("Let 'Em Eat Cake")

Registration 5
Rhythm: Swing or Jazz

Words by Ira Gershwin
Music by George Gershwin

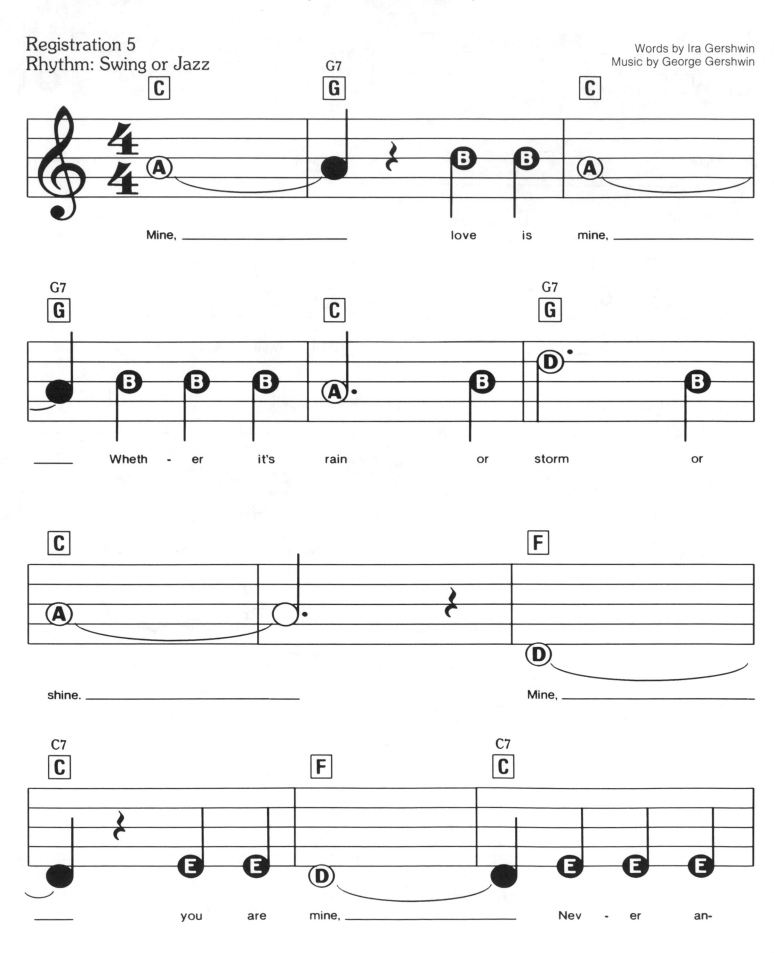

97

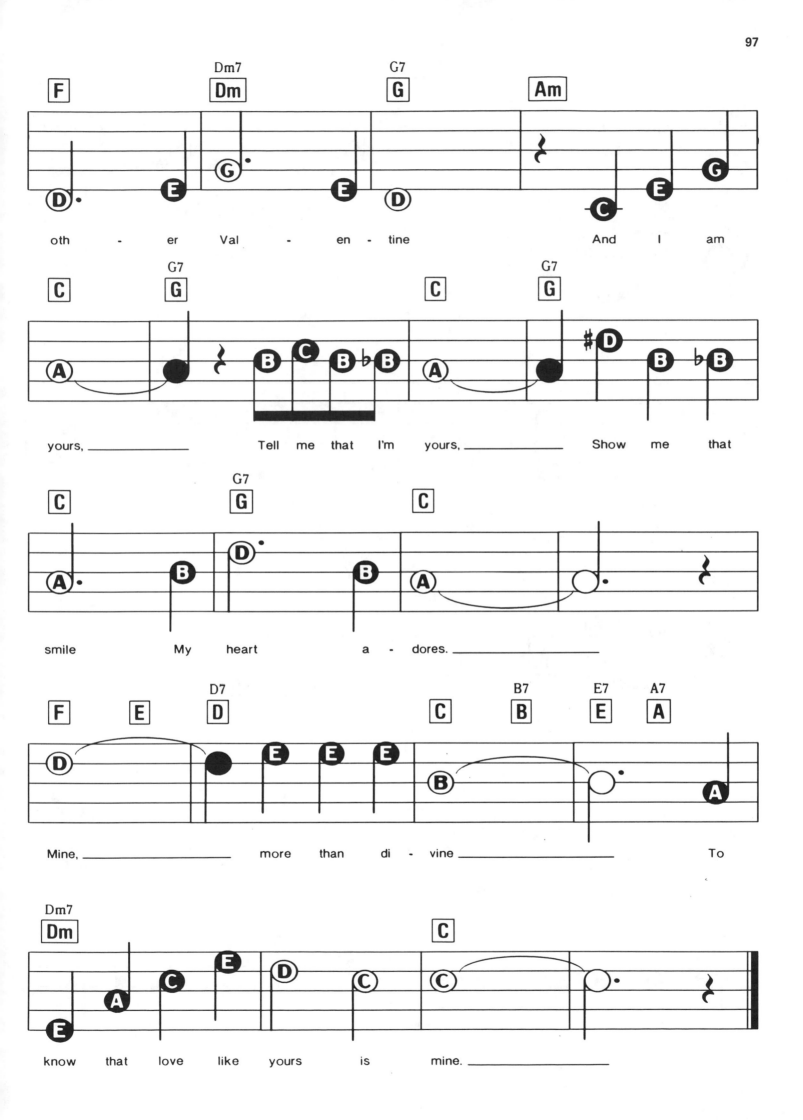

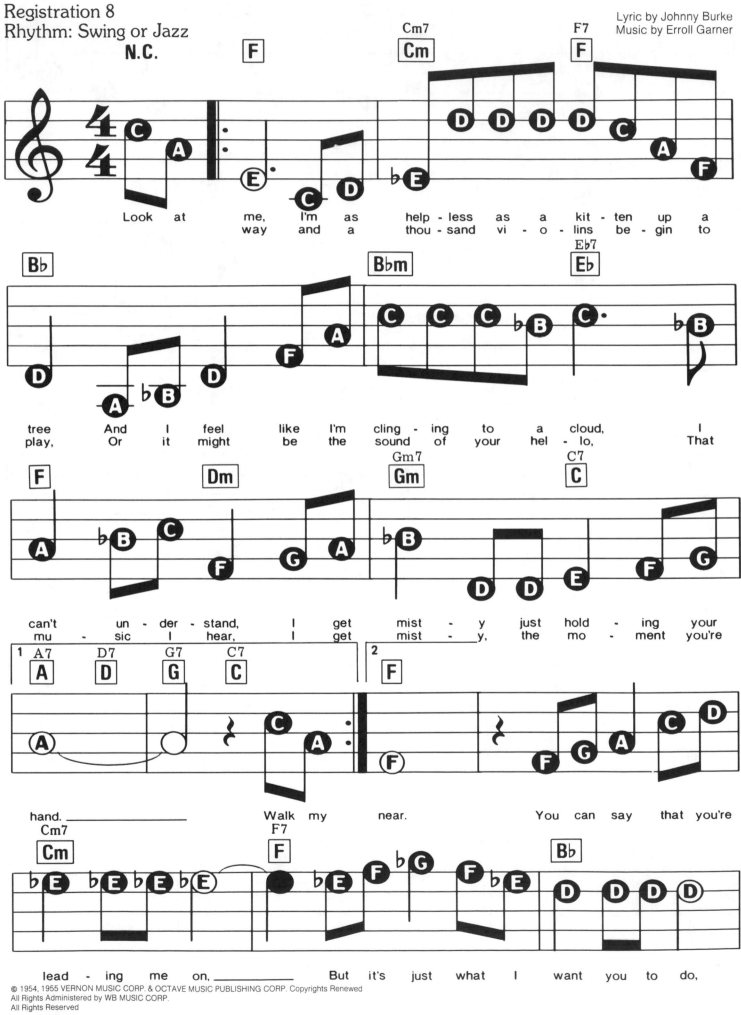

Misty

Registration 8
Rhythm: Swing or Jazz

Lyric by Johnny Burke
Music by Erroll Garner

New York, New York

Registration 8
Rhythm: Swing or Jazz

Words by Betty Comden and Adolph Green
Music by Leonard Bernstein

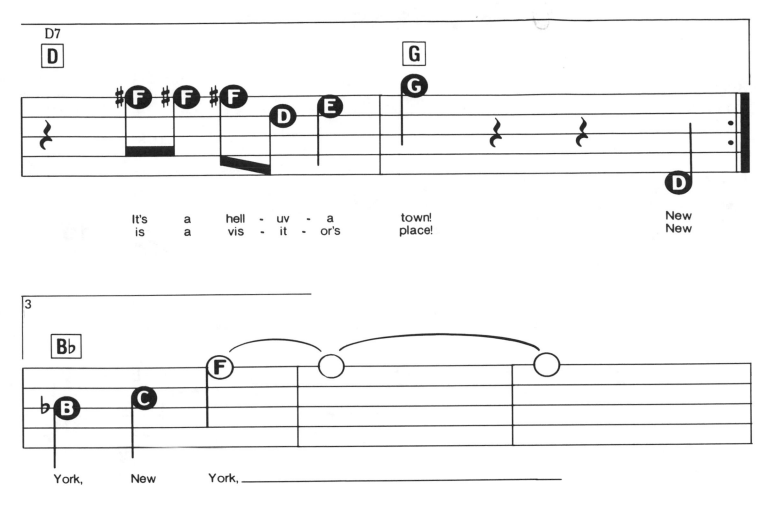

It's a hell - uv - a town!
is a vis - it - or's place!

New
New

York, New York, _____

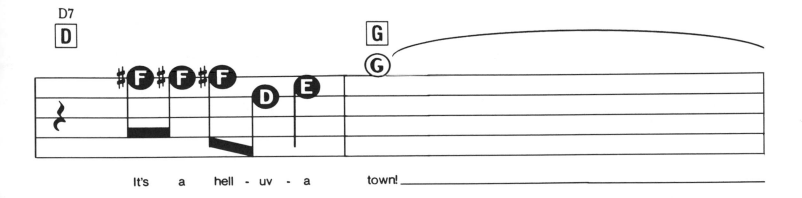

It's a hell - uv - a town! _____

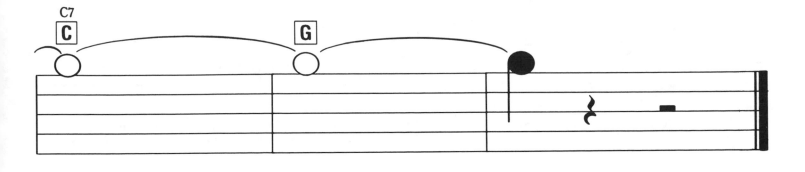

On Broadway

Registration 7
Rhythm: Rock

Words and Music by Barry Mann,
Cynthia Weil, Mike Stoller
and Jerry Leiber

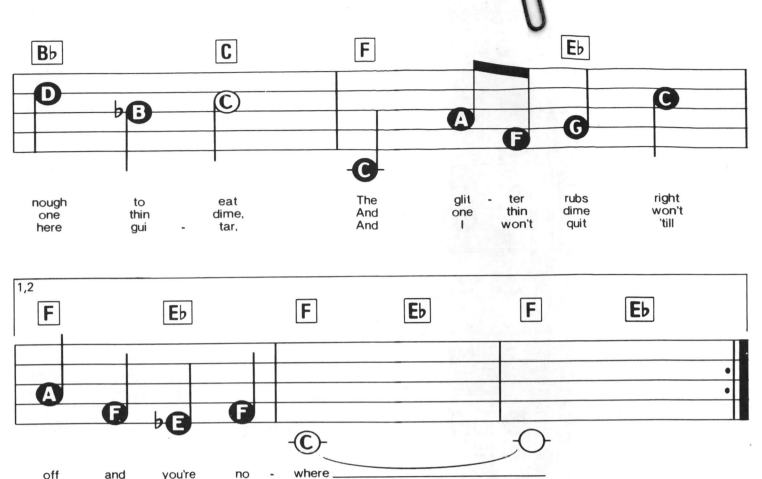

nough   to   eat   The   glit - ter   rubs   right
one   thin   dime,   And   one   thin   dime   won't
here   gui - tar,   And   I   won't   quit   'till

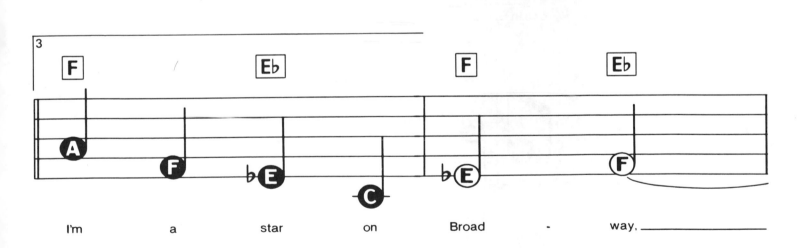

off   and   you're   no - where
e - ven   shine   your   shoes.

I'm   a   star   on   Broad - way,

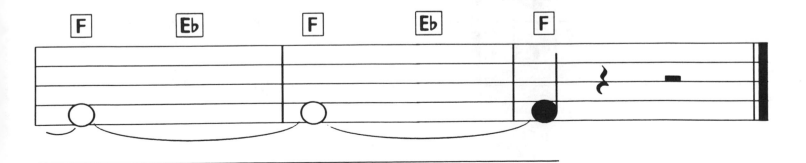

Paloma Blanca

Registration 1
Rhythm: Latin or Bossa Nova

Words and Music by
Hans Bouwens

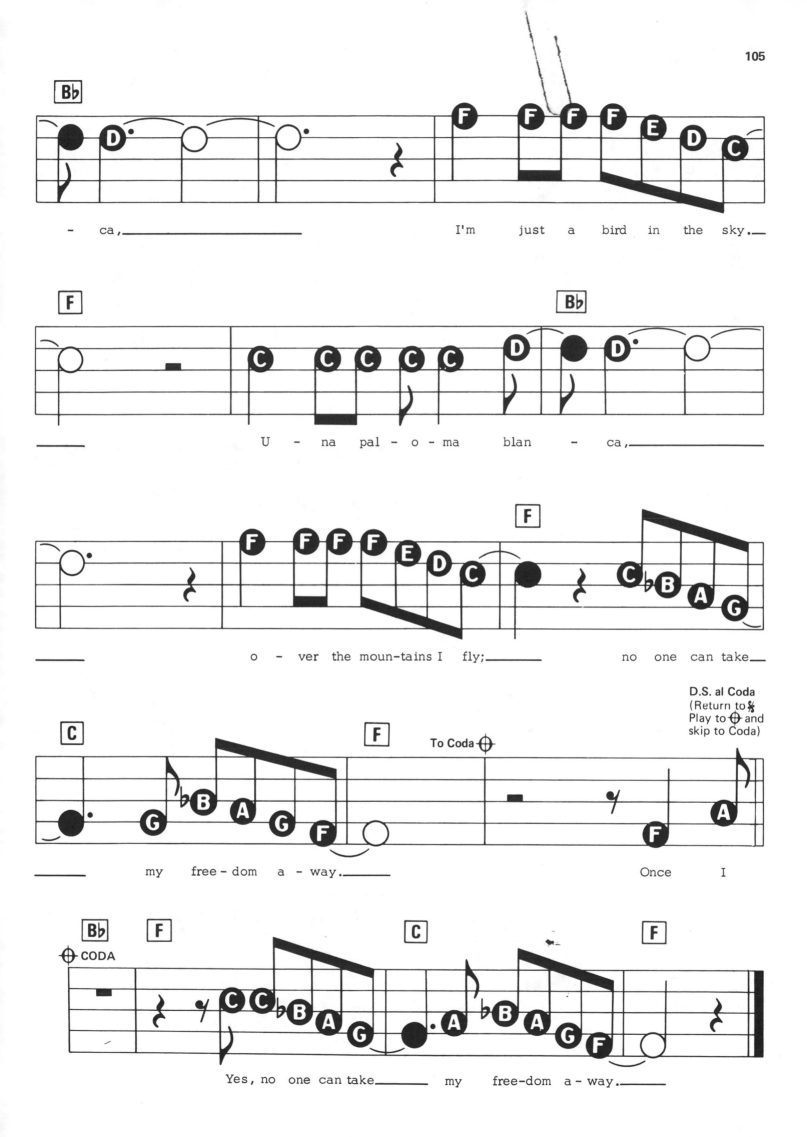

Put Your Hand In The Hand

Registration 8
Rhythm: Rock or Jazz Rock

Words and Music by
Gene MacLellan

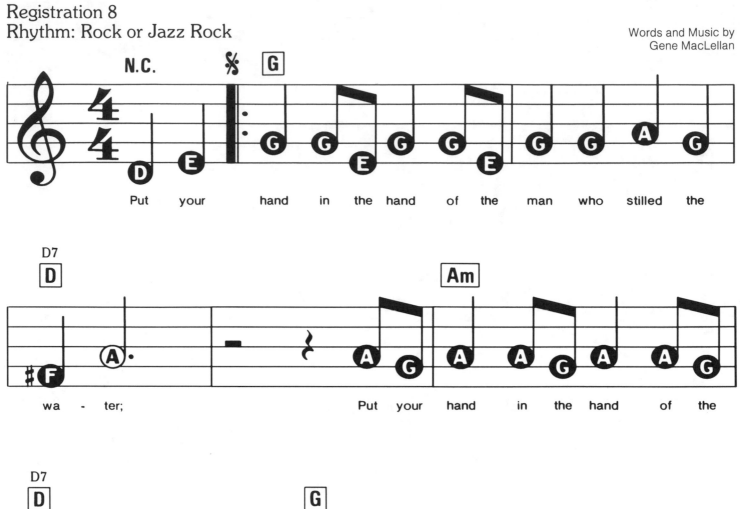

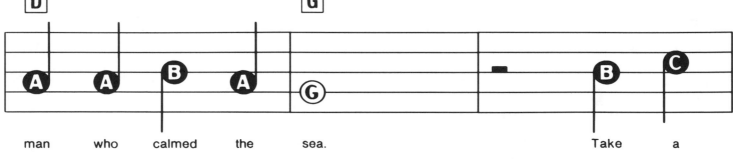

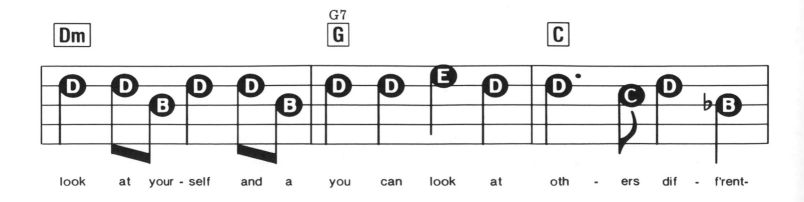

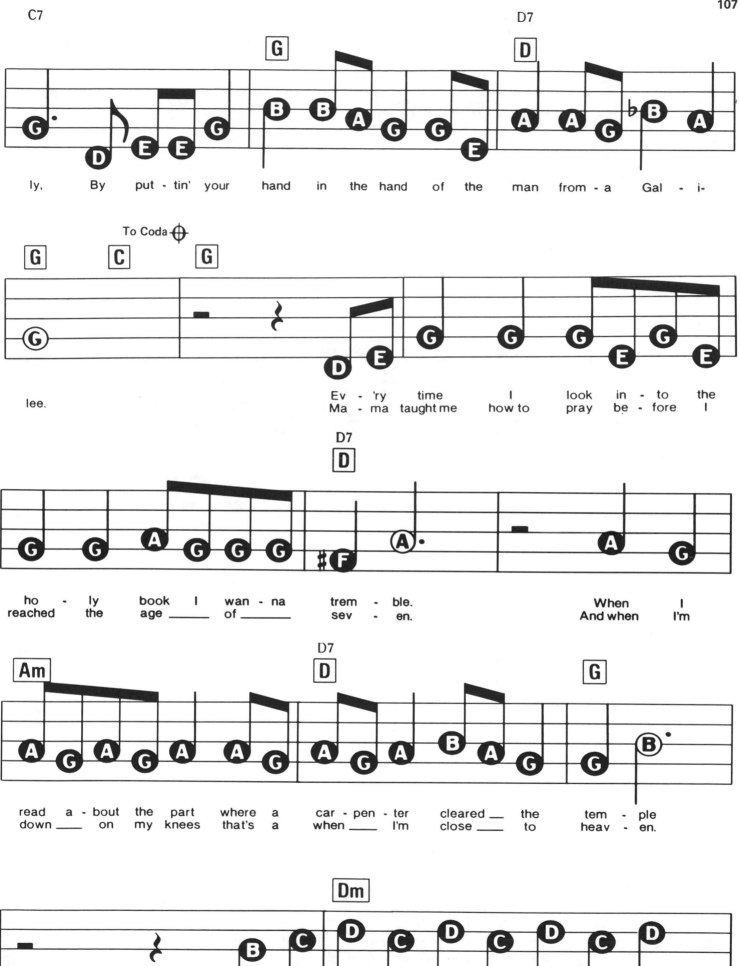

ly, By put - tin' your hand in the hand of the man from - a Gal - i-

lee.

Ev - 'ry time I look in - to the
Ma - ma taught me how to pray be - fore I

ho - ly book I wan - na trem - ble. When I
reached the age ____ of ____ sev - en. And when I'm

read a - bout the part where a car - pen - ter cleared __ the tem - ple
down ___ on my knees that's a when ___ I'm close ___ to heav - en.

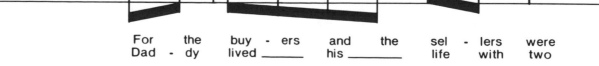

For the buy - ers and the sel - lers were
Dad - dy lived ____ his ____ life with two

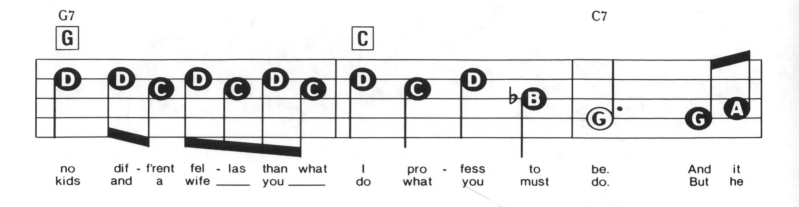

no dif - f'rent fel - las than what I pro - fess to be. And it
kids and a wife ___ you ___ do what you must do. But he

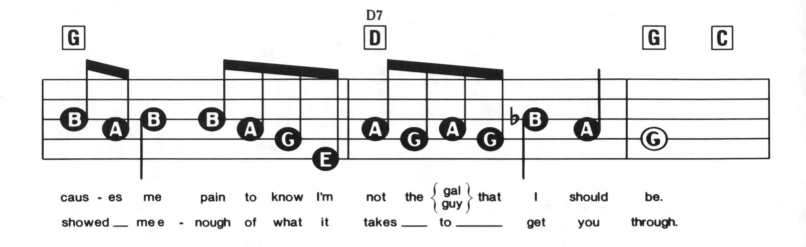

caus - es me pain to know I'm not the { gal / guy } that I should be.
showed ___ me e - nough of what it takes ___ to ___ get you through.

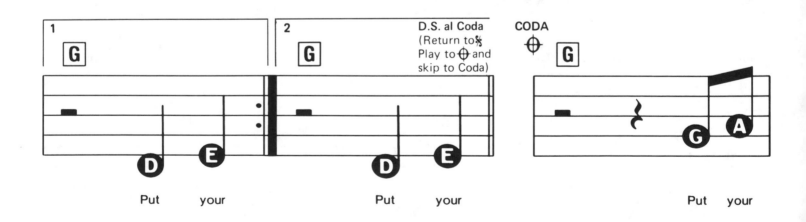

1
Put your

2
D.S. al Coda
(Return to %
Play to ⊕ and
skip to Coda)
Put your

CODA ⊕
Put your

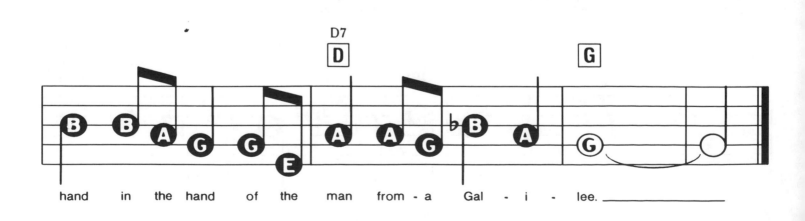

hand in the hand of the man from - a Gal - i - lee. ___

The Rose

(From the Twentieth Century-Fox Motion Picture Release "THE ROSE")

Registration 5
Rhythm: Rock or Slow Rock

Words and Music by
Amanda McBroom

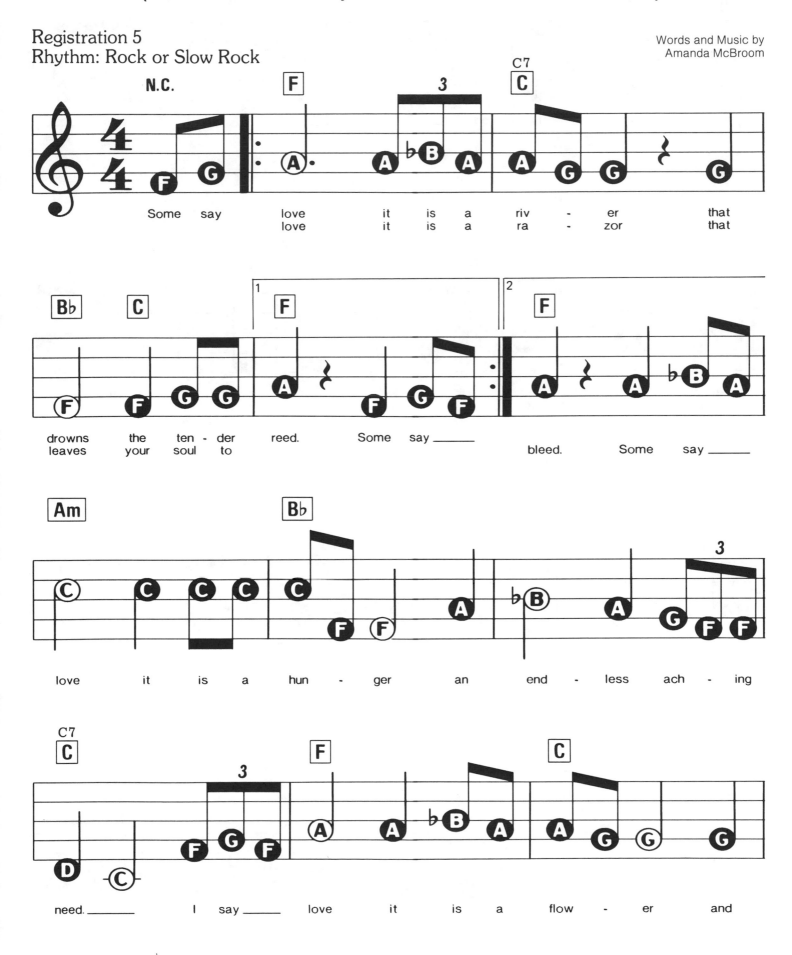

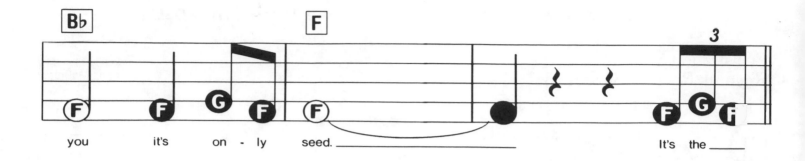

you it's on - ly seed. _____ It's the _____

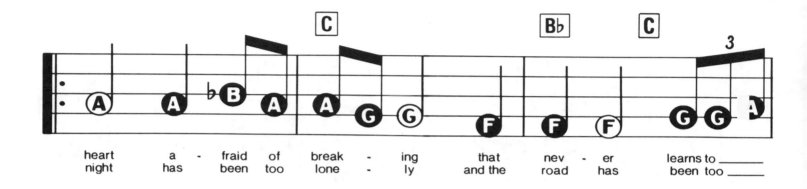

heart a - fraid of break - ing that nev - er learns to _____
night has been too lone - ly and the road has been too _____

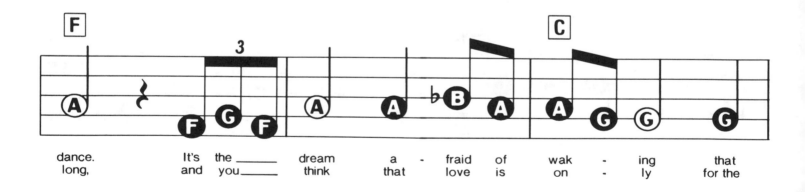

dance. It's the _____ dream a - fraid of wak - ing that
long, and you_____ think that love is on - ly that for the

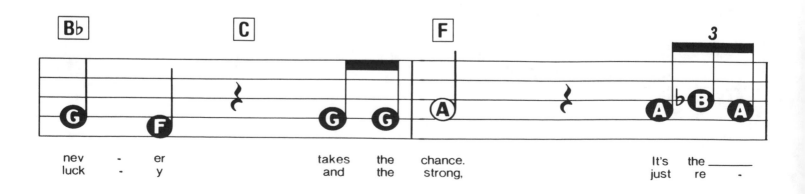

nev - er takes the chance. It's the _____
luck - y and the strong, just re -

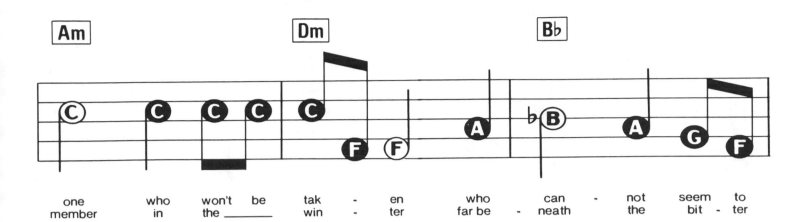

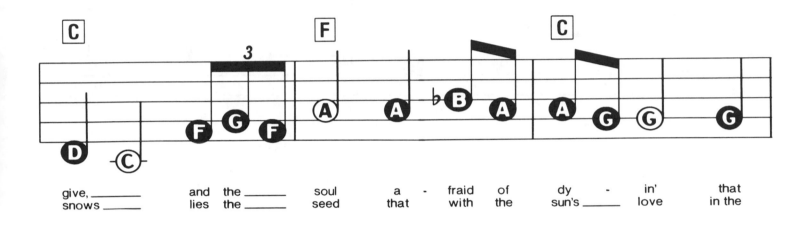

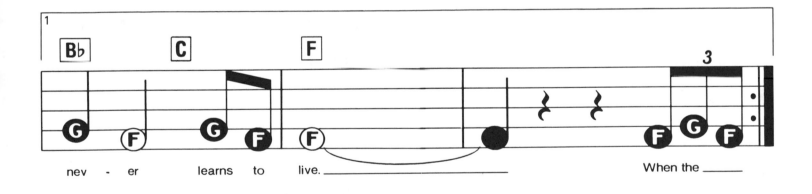

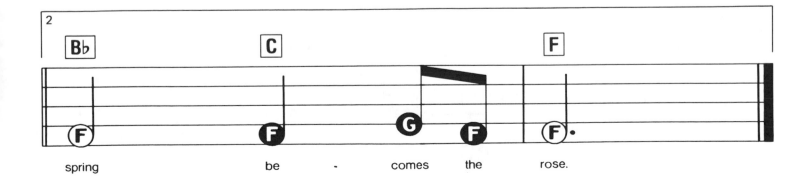

'Round Midnight

Words by Bernie Hanighen
Music by Cootie Williams and Thelonious Monk

Registration 4
Rhythm: Swing or Jazz

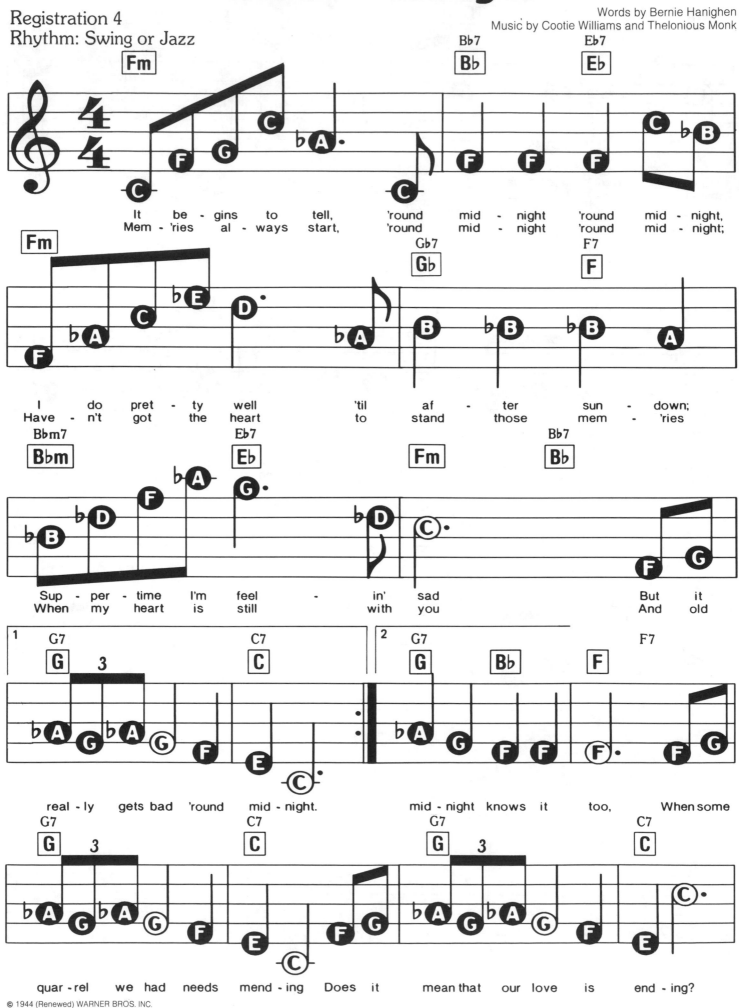

It be-gins to tell, 'round mid-night 'round mid-night,
Mem-'ries al-ways start, 'round mid-night 'round mid-night;

I do pret-ty well, 'til af-ter sun-down;
Have-n't got the heart to stand those mem-'ries

Sup-per-time I'm feel-in' sad But it
When my heart is still with you And old

real-ly gets bad 'round mid-night.
mid-night knows it too, When some

quar-rel we had needs mend-ing Does it mean that our love is end-ing?

112

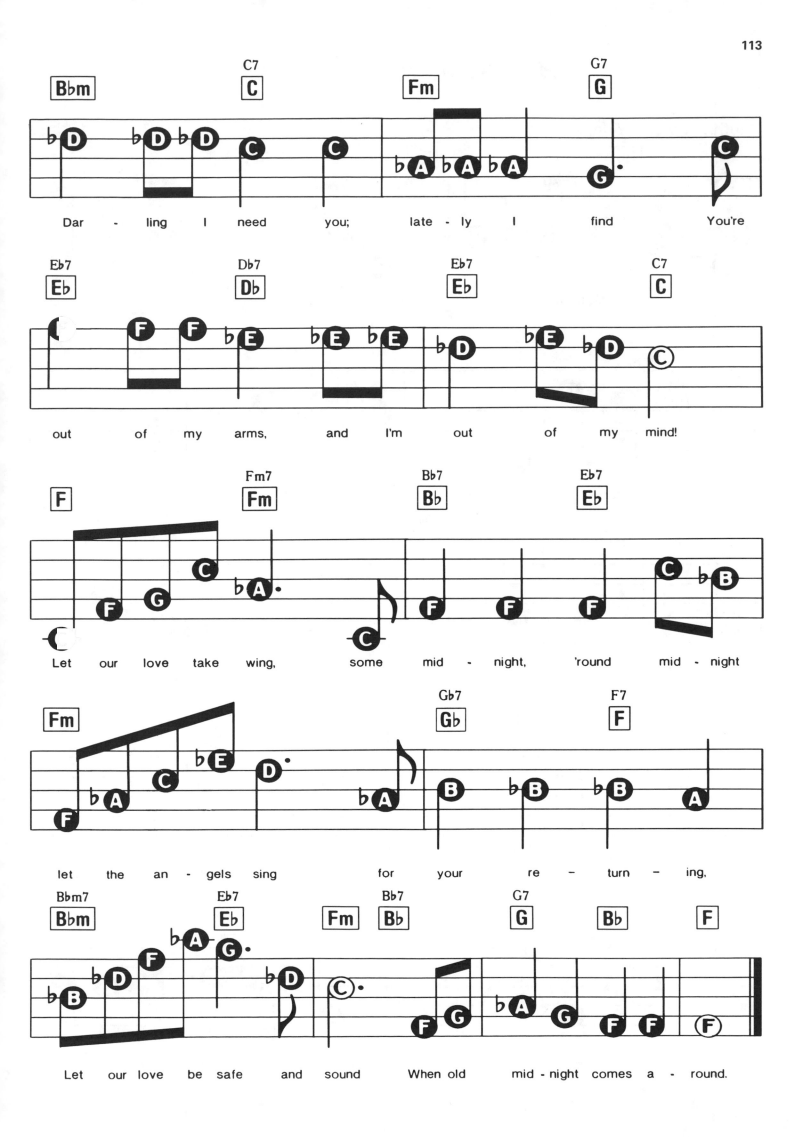

Scotch And Soda

Registration 8
Rhythm: Swing or Jazz

Words and Music by
Dave Guard

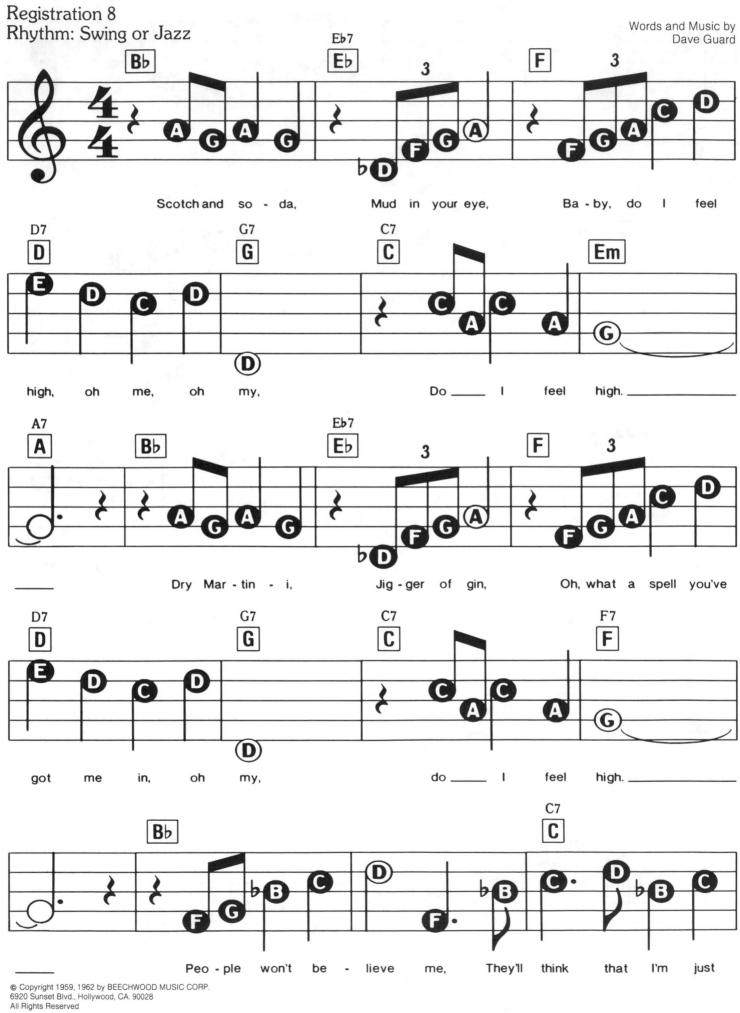

115

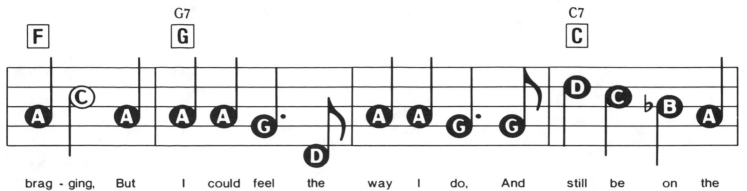

brag - ging, But I could feel the way I do, And still be on the

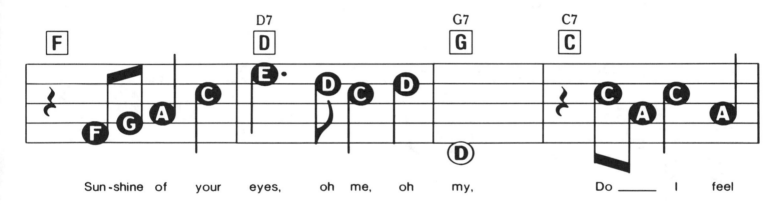

wa - gon. All I need is one of your smiles,

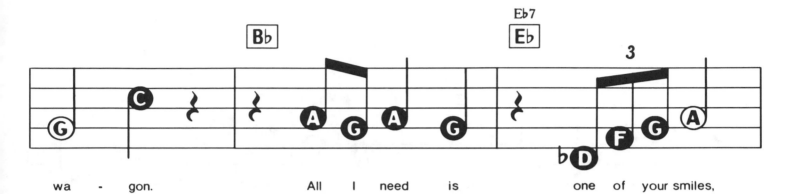

Sun -shine of your eyes, oh me, oh my, Do ____ I feel

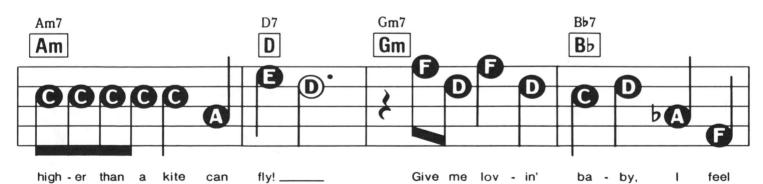

high - er than a kite can fly! ____ Give me lov - in' ba - by, I feel

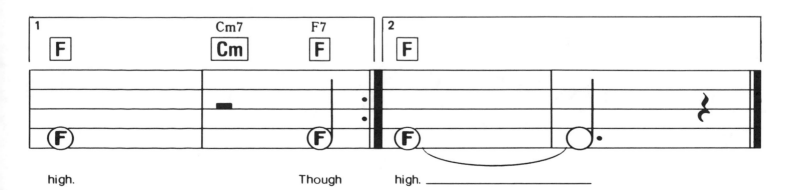

high. Though high. _____

Shine On Your Shoes

Registration 4
Rhythm: Fox Trot or Swing

Words and Music by
Howard Dietz and Arthur Schwartz

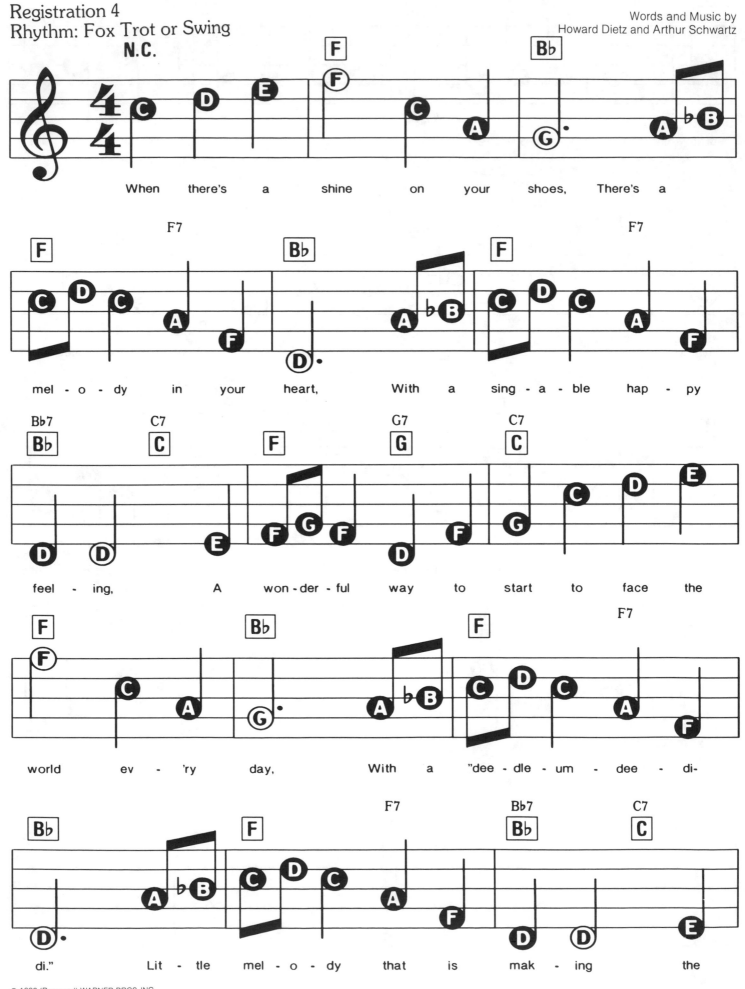

When there's a shine on your shoes, There's a
mel - o - dy in your heart, With a sing - a - ble hap - py
feel - ing, A won - der - ful way to start to face the
world ev - 'ry day, With a "dee - dle - um - dee - di -
di." Lit - tle mel - o - dy that is mak - ing the

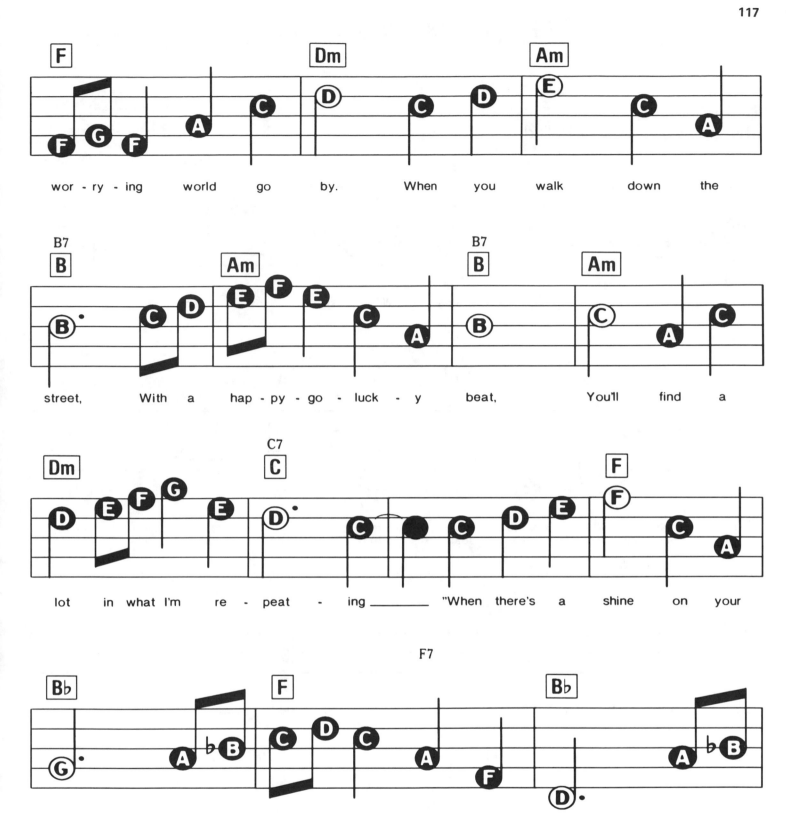

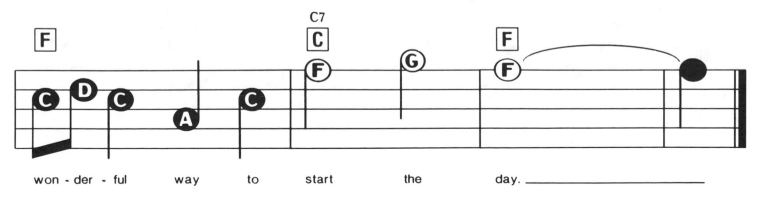

Softly As In A Morning Sunrise

Registration 10
Rhythm: Slow Rock or Ballad

Words by Oscar Hammerstein II
Music by Sigmund Romberg

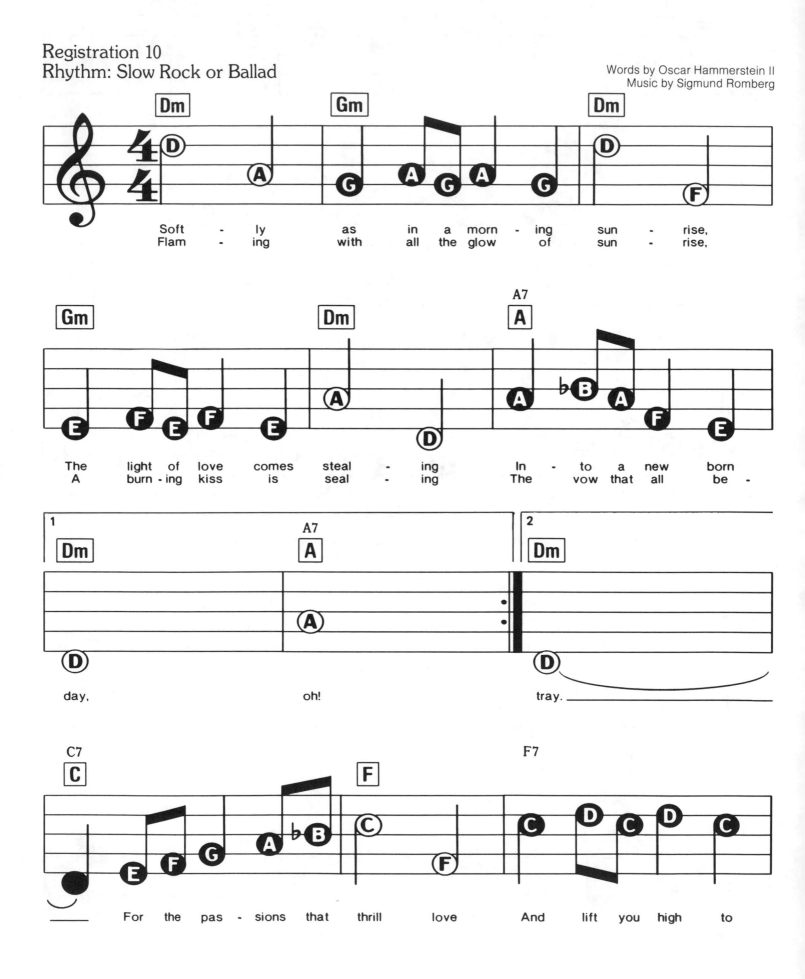

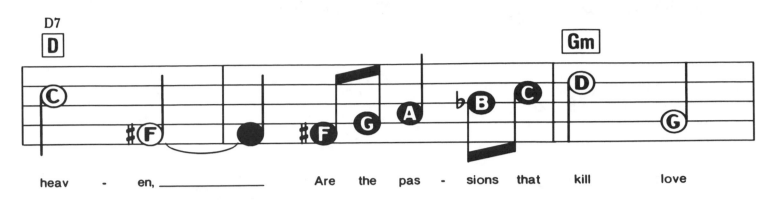

heav - en, _____ Are the pas - sions that kill love

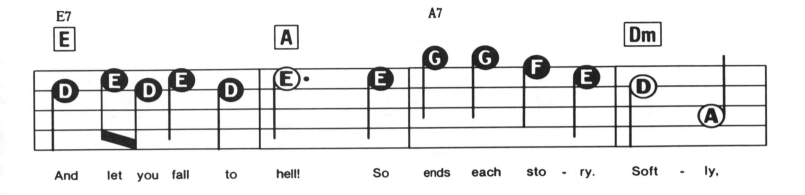

And let you fall to hell! So ends each sto - ry. Soft - ly,

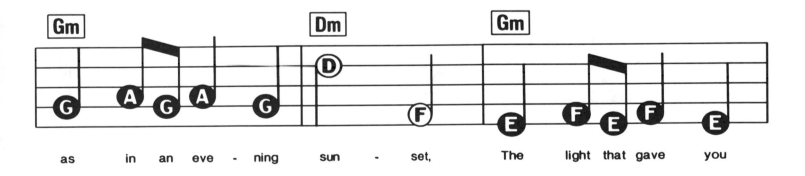

as in an eve - ning sun - set, The light that gave you

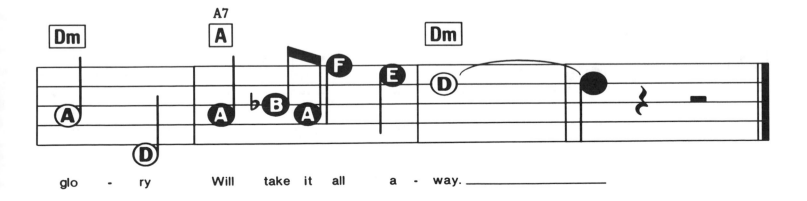

glo - ry Will take it all a - way. _____

Something To Remember You By

Registration 2
Rhythm: Fox Trot or Ballad

Words by Howard Dietz
Music by Arthur Schwartz

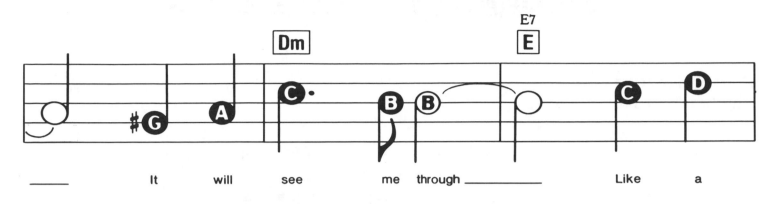

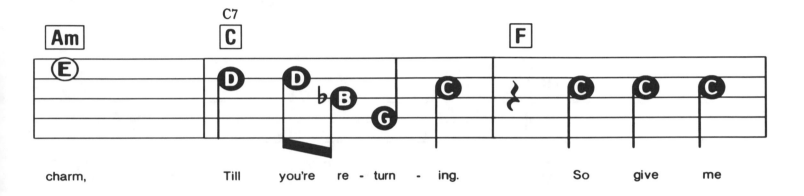

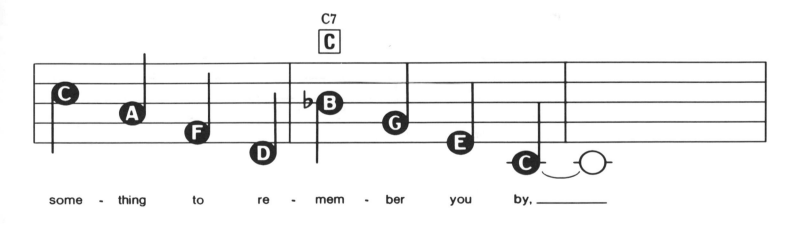

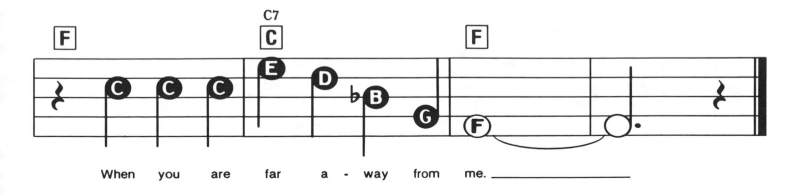

Something's Gotta Give

Registration 5
Rhythm: Fox Trot or Swing

Words and Music by
Johnny Mercer

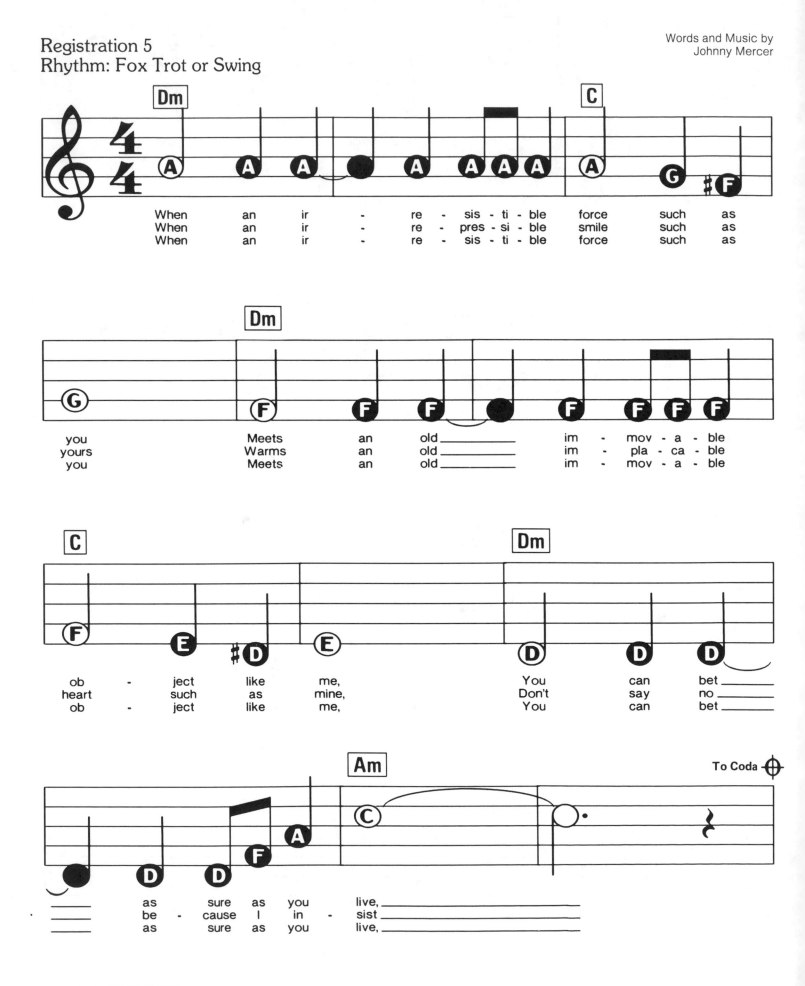

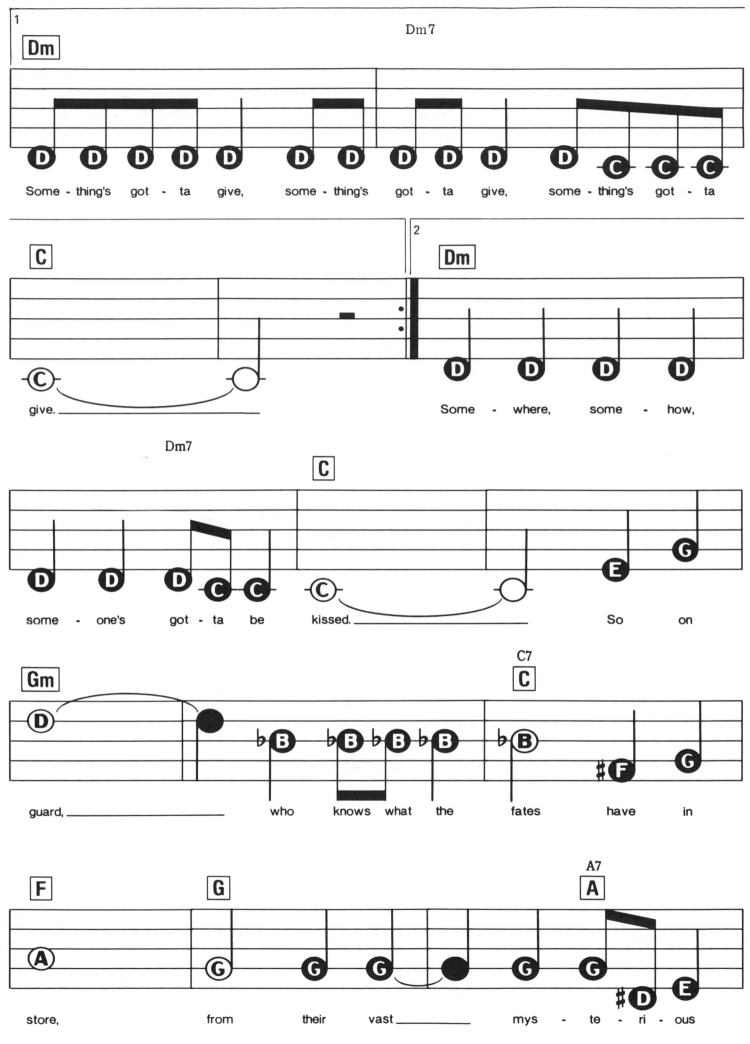

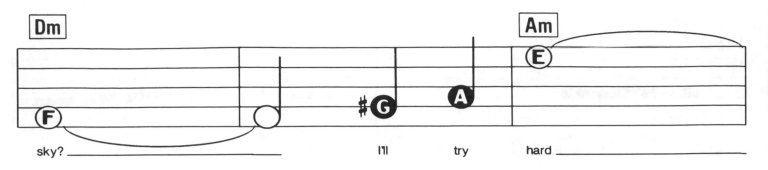

sky? _____   I'll   try   hard _____

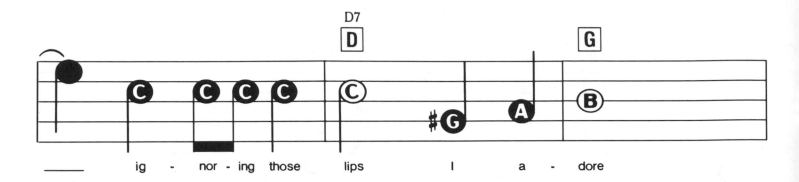

___   ig - nor - ing   those   lips   I   a - dore

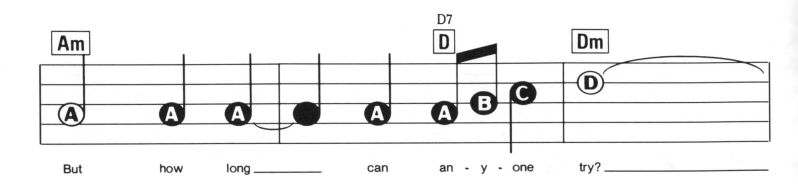

But   how   long _____   can   an - y - one   try? _____

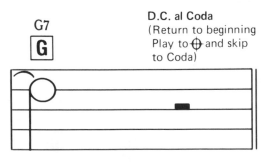

D.C. al Coda
(Return to beginning
Play to ⊕ and skip
to Coda)

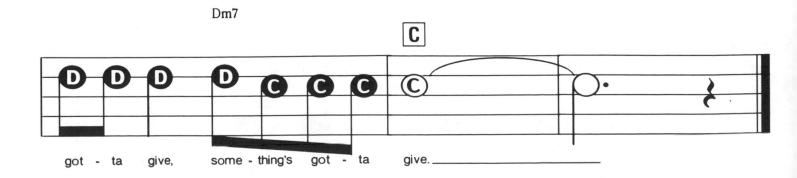

some - thing's   got - ta   give,   some - thing's

got - ta   give,   some - thing's   got - ta   give. _____

Spanish Eyes

Registration 3
Rhythm: Latin or Bossa Nova

Words by Charles Singleton and Eddie Snyder
Music by Bert Kaempfert

126

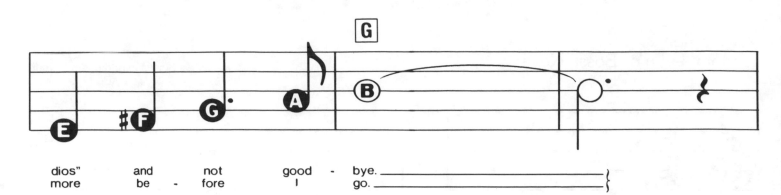

dios" and not good - bye. _____
more be - fore I go. _____

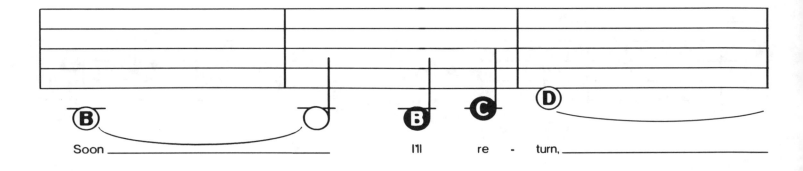

Soon _____ I'll re - turn, _____

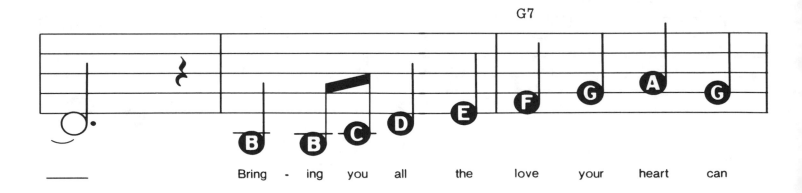

Bring - ing you all the love your heart can

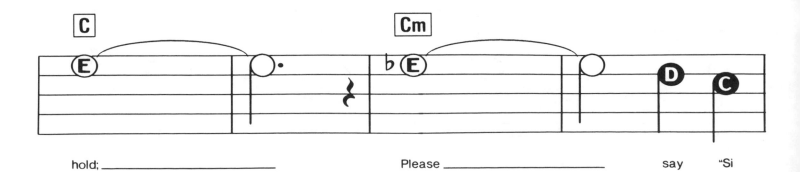

hold; _____ Please _____ say "Si

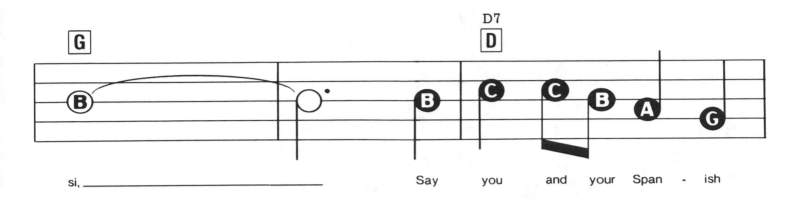

si, _____ Say you and your Span - ish

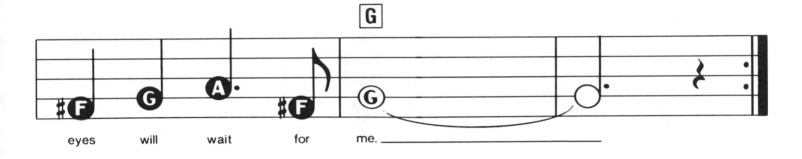

eyes will wait for me. _____

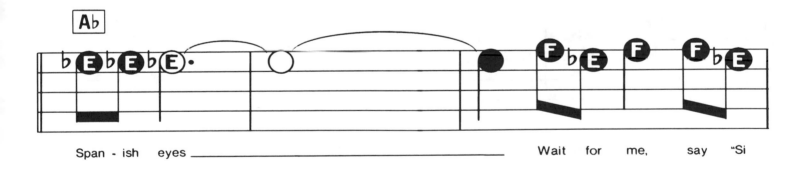

Span - ish eyes _____ Wait for me, say "Si

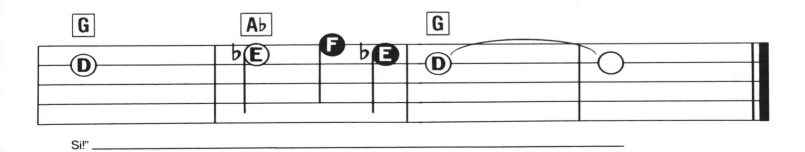

Si!" _____

Sukiyaki
(My First Lonely Night)

Words and Music by
Hachidai Nakamura and Rokusuke El
English Lyric by
Tom Leslie and Buzz Cason

Registration 4
Rhythm: Country or Shuffle

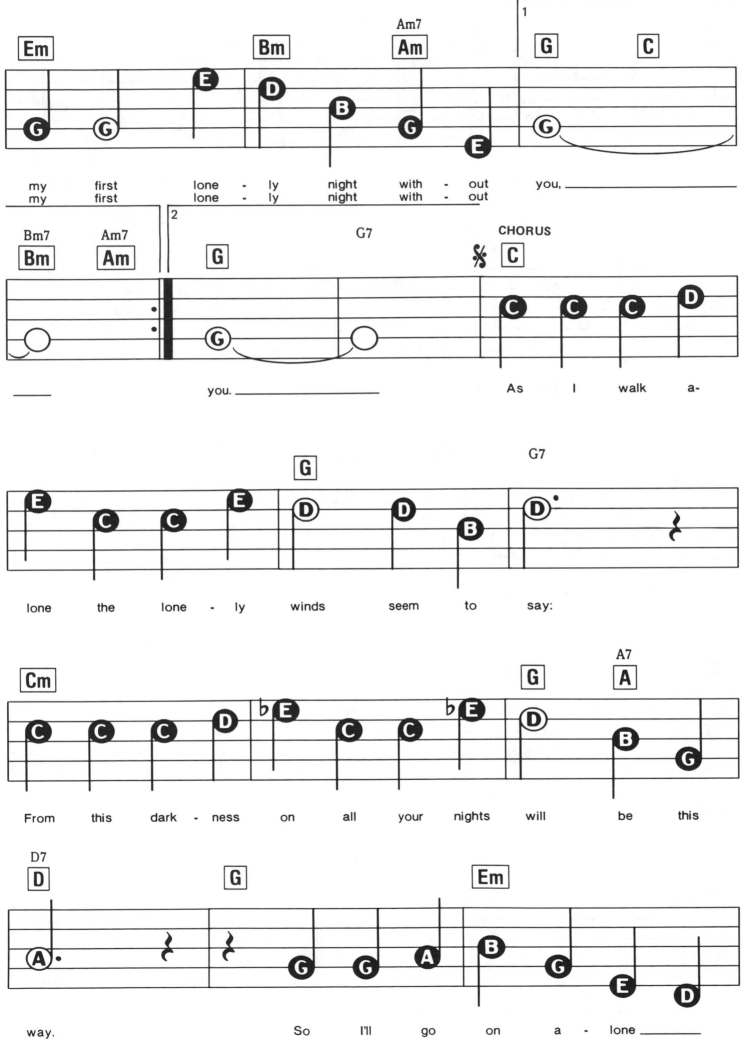

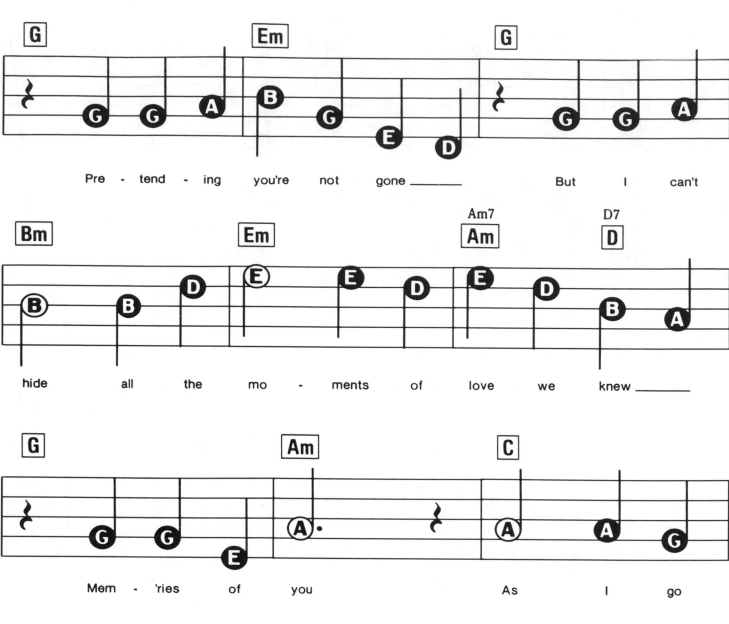

Pre - tend - ing you're not gone _____ But I can't

hide all the mo - ments of love we knew _____

Mem - 'ries of you As I go

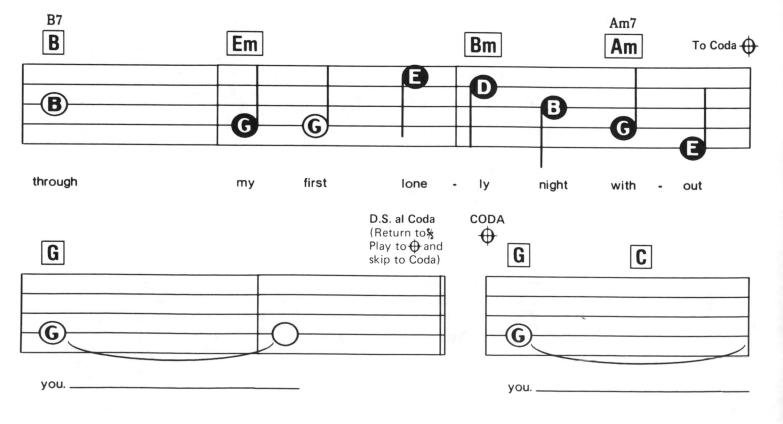

through my first lone - ly night with - out

D.S. al Coda
(Return to %
Play to ⊕ and
skip to Coda)

CODA
⊕

you. _____

you. _____

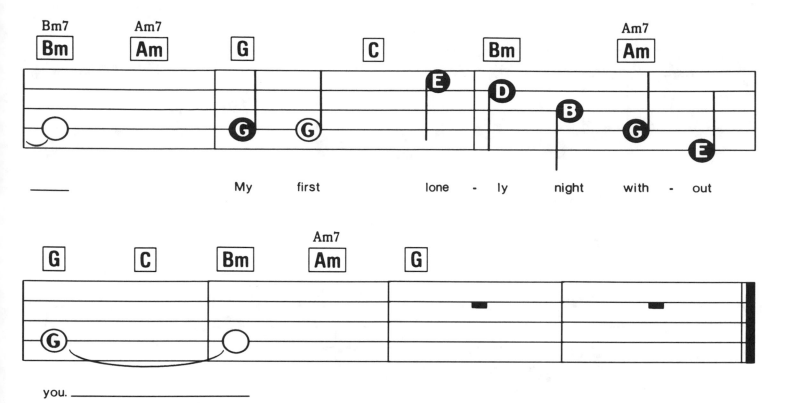

My first lone - ly night with - out

you. _____

Japenese Lyrics

Verse 1   UEO MUITE ARUKO NAMIDAGA KODORF MAI YO NI
            ONOIDASU HARUNOHI HITORI POCHINO YORU
            UEO MUITE ARUKO NIJINDA HASHIO KASO ETA
            ONOIDASU NATAUNO HI HITOTI POCHINO YORU

Chorus 1   SHIAWASEWA KUMONO UENI
            SHIAWASEWA KUMONO UENI
            UEO MUITE ARUKO NAMIDAGA KOPO RE MAI YONI
            NAKINAGARA ARUKU HITORI POCHINO YORU

Chorus 2   KANASHIMWN HOSHINO KAGENI
            KANASHIMIWA TAUKINO KAGENI
            UEO MUITE ARUKO NAMIDAGA KODO RE MAI YONI
            NAKINAGARA ARUKU HITORI POCHINO YORU
            HITORI POCHINO YORU

Summer Me, Winter Me

(Theme from "Piscasso Summer")

Registration 10
Rhythm: Slow Rock or Ballad

Words by Alan Marilyn Bergman
Music by Michel Legrand

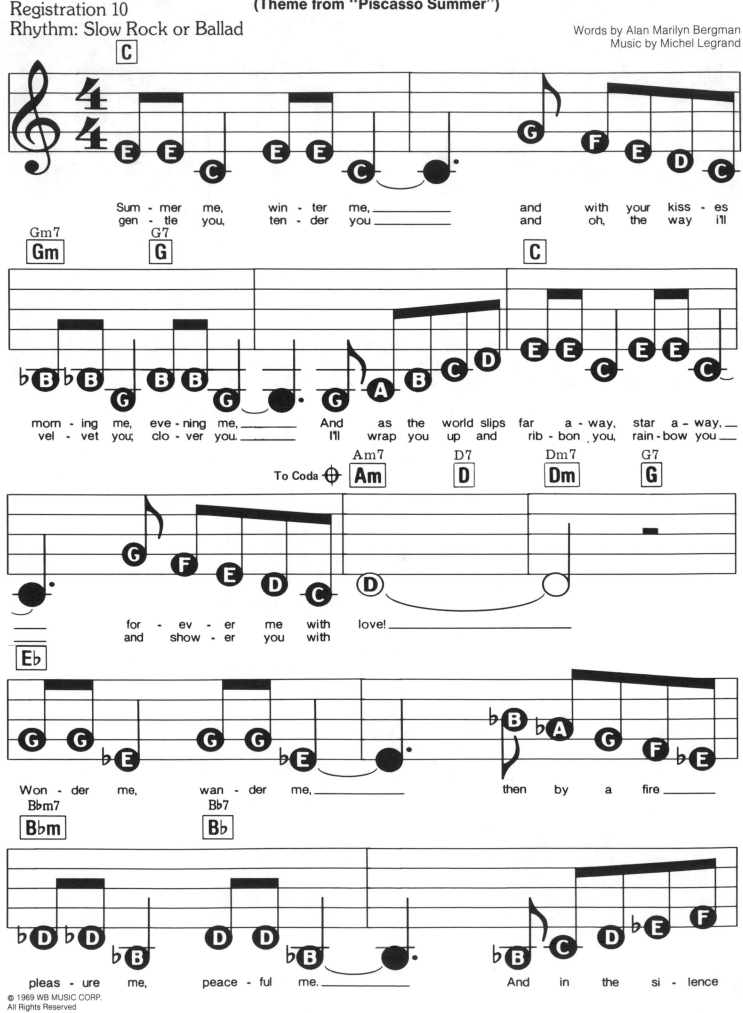

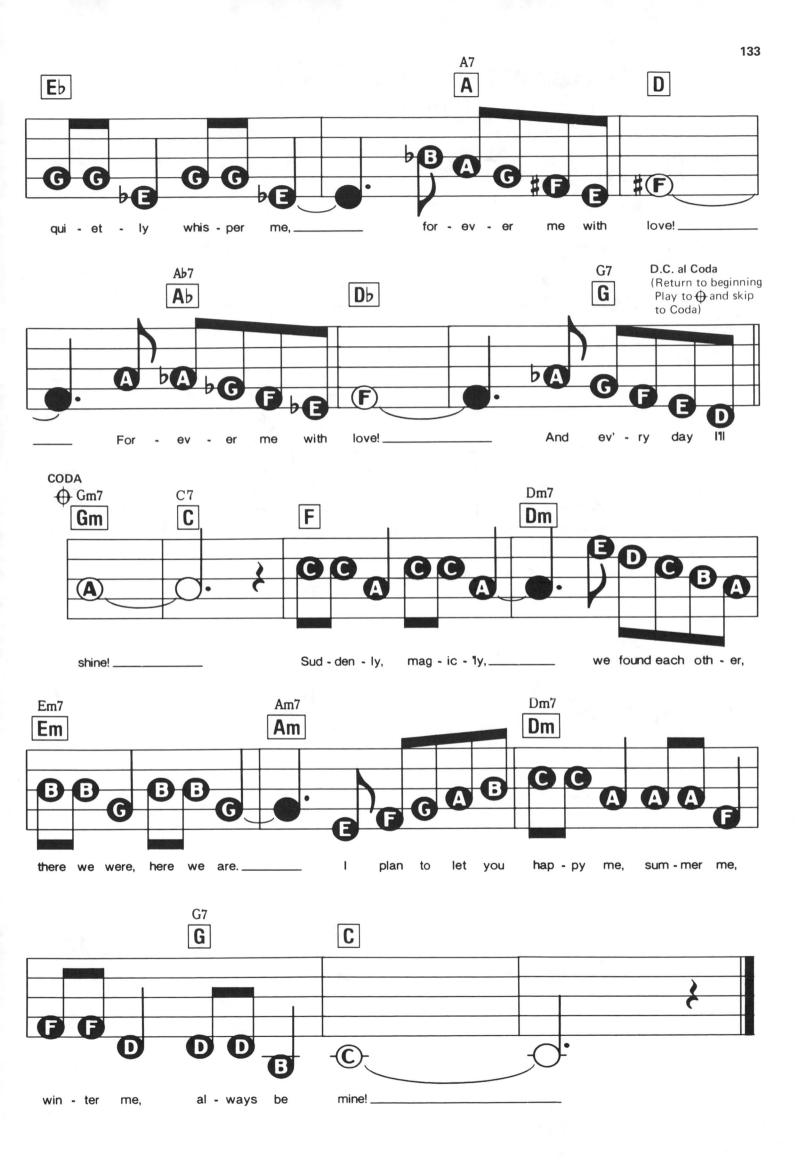

There's A Kind Of Hush
(All Over The World)

Registration 3
Rhythm: Rock or Slow Rock

Words and Music by
Les Reed and Geoff Stephens

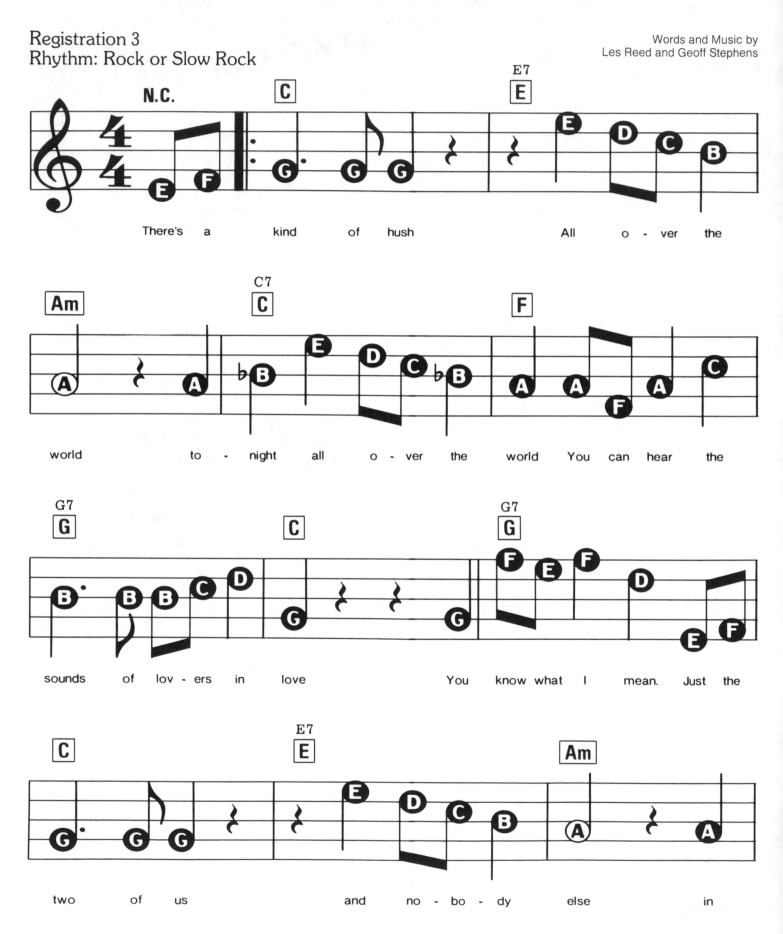

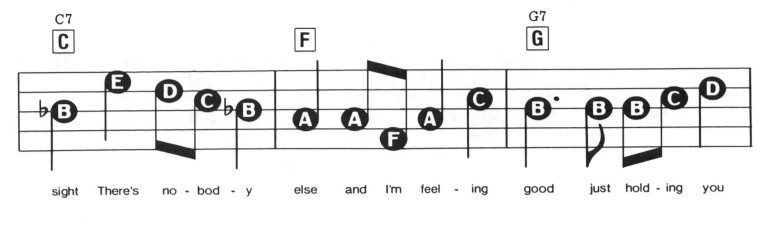

sight There's no - bod - y else and I'm feel - ing good just hold - ing you

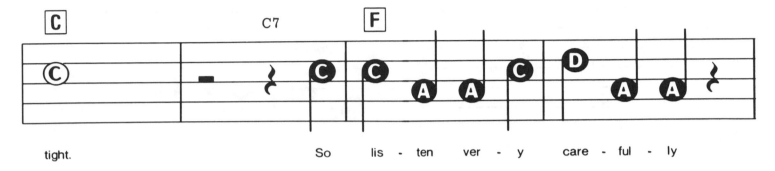

tight.   So lis - ten ver - y care - ful - ly

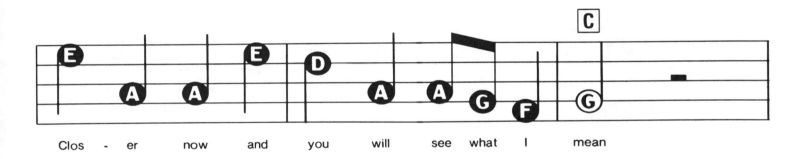

Clos - er now and you will see what I mean

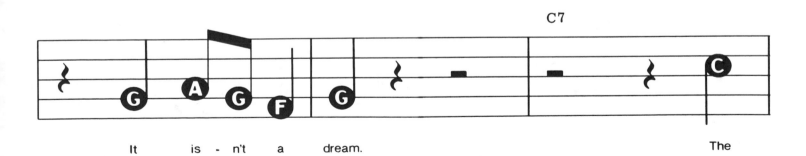

It is - n't a dream.   The

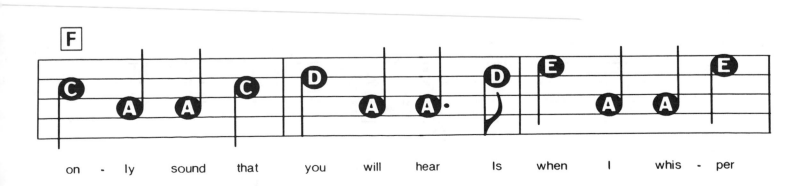

on - ly sound that you will hear Is when I whis - per

136

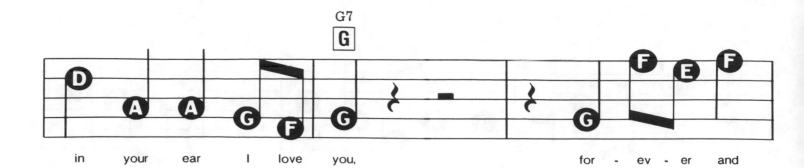

in your ear I love you,   for - ev - er and

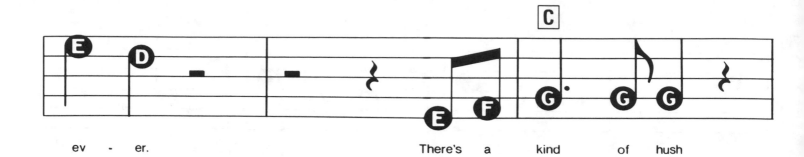

ev - er.   There's a kind of hush

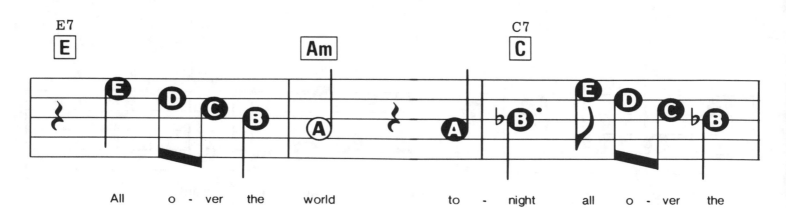

All o - ver the world   to - night all o - ver the

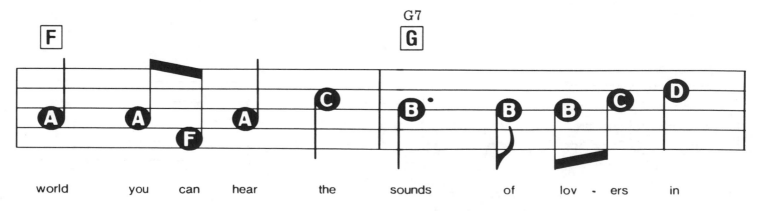

world you can hear the sounds of lov - ers in

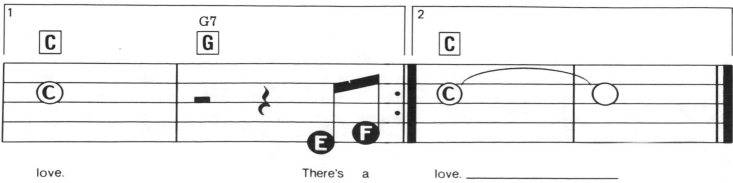

love.   There's a   love. _____

Thine Alone

Words by Henry Blossom
Music by Victor Herbert

Registration 3
Rhythm: Fox Trot or Ballad

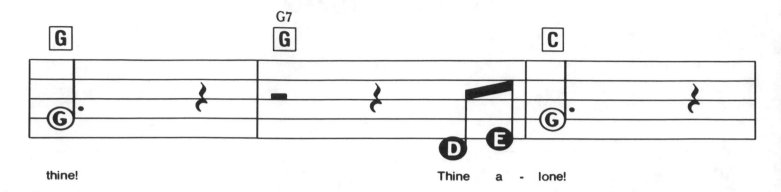

thine!   Thine   a - lone!

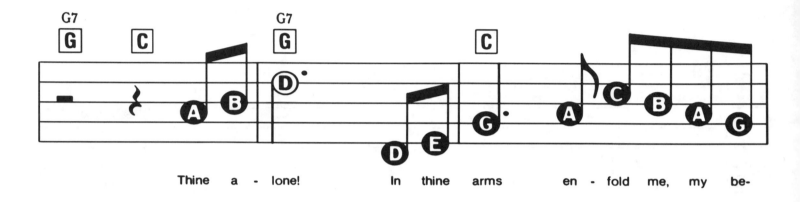

Thine   a - lone!   In   thine   arms   en - fold   me,   my   be-

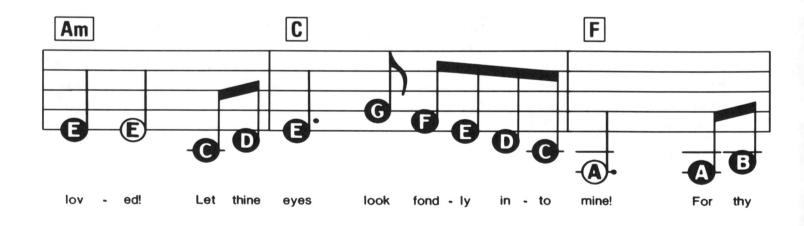

lov   - ed!   Let   thine   eyes   look   fond - ly   in - to   mine!   For   thy

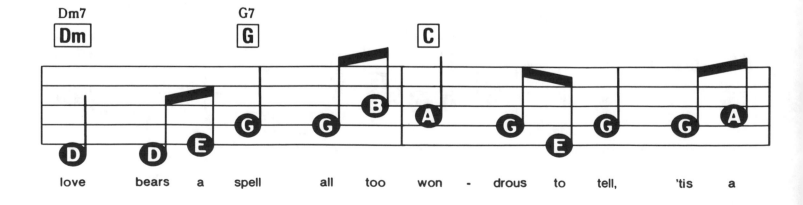

love   bears   a   spell   all   too   won - drous   to   tell,   'tis   a

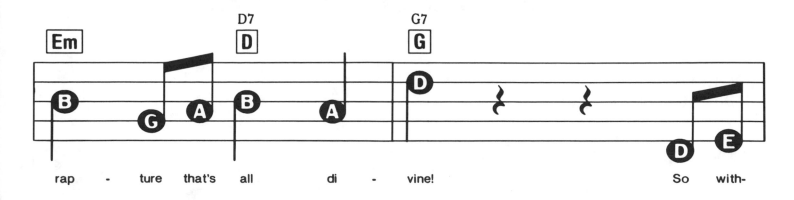

rap - ture that's all di - vine! So with-

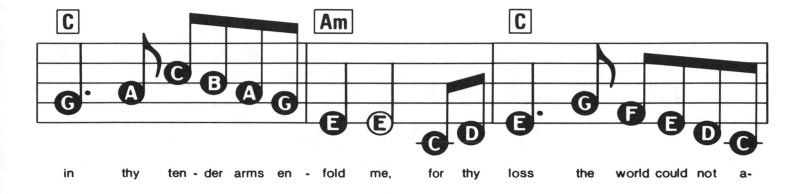

in thy ten - der arms en - fold me, for thy loss the world could not a-

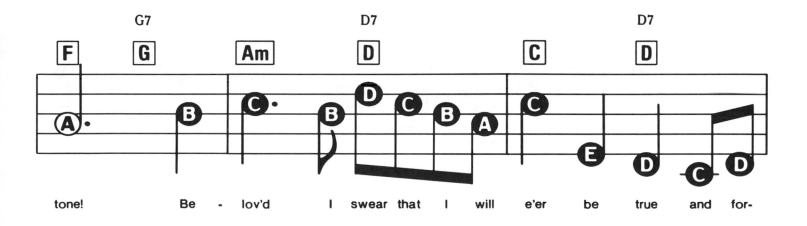

tone! Be - lov'd I swear that I will e'er be true and for-

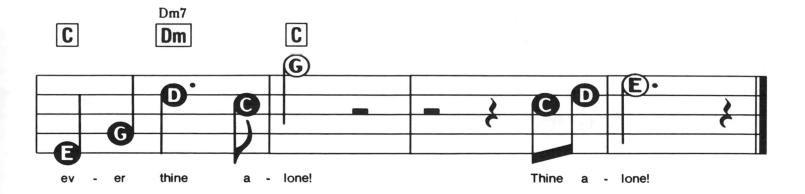

ev - er thine a - lone! Thine a - lone!

This Heart Of Mine

Registration 8
Rhythm: Country or Shuffle

Words and Music by
Robert Miller & Barrett Strong

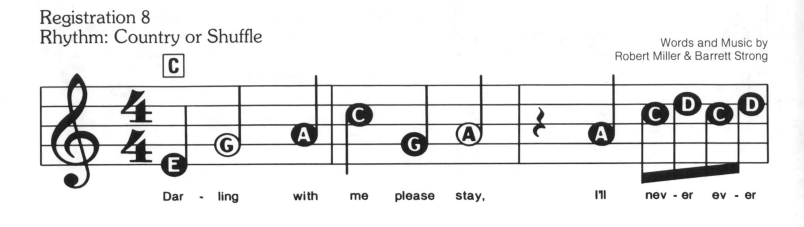

Dar - ling with me please stay, I'll nev - er ev - er

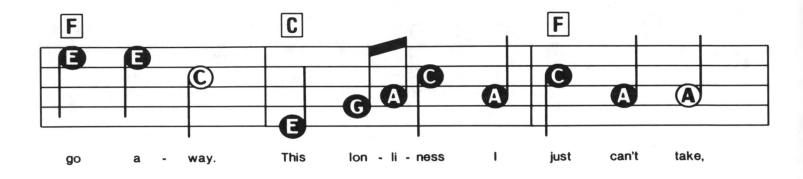

go a - way. This lon - li - ness I just can't take,

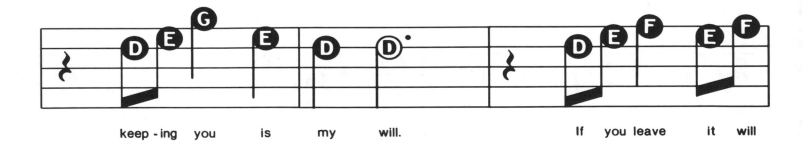

keep - ing you is my will. If you leave it will

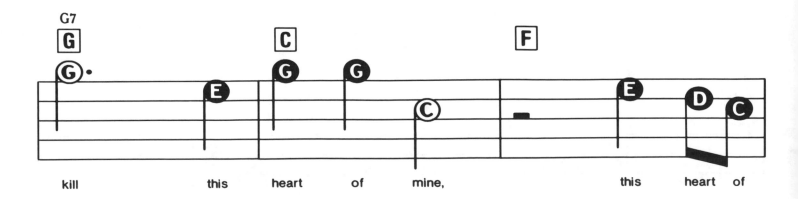

kill this heart of mine, this heart of

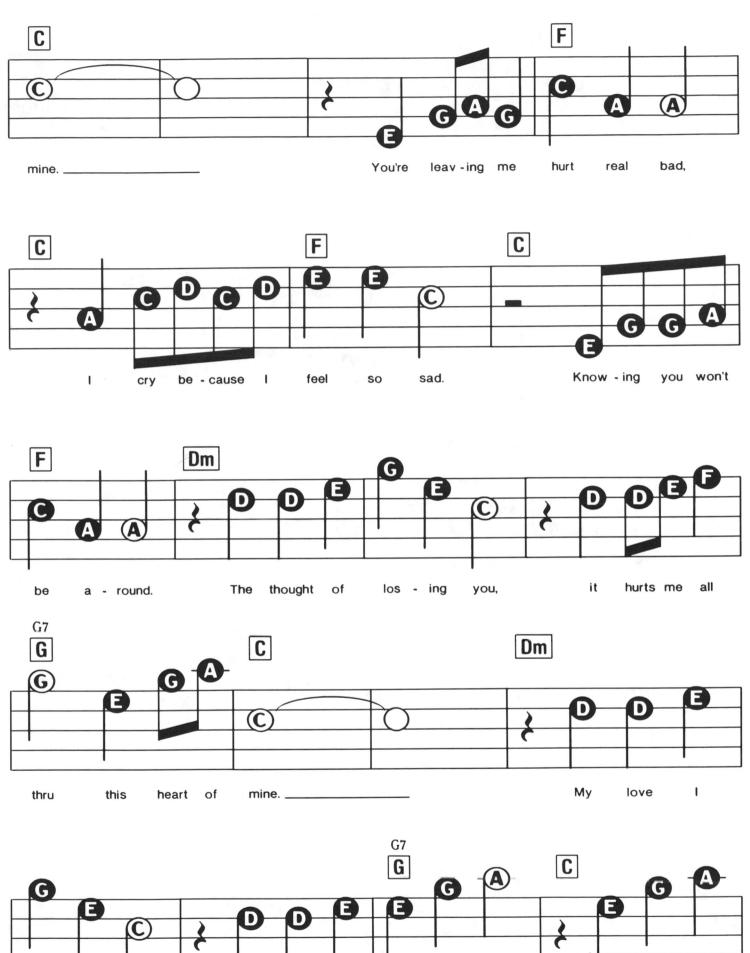

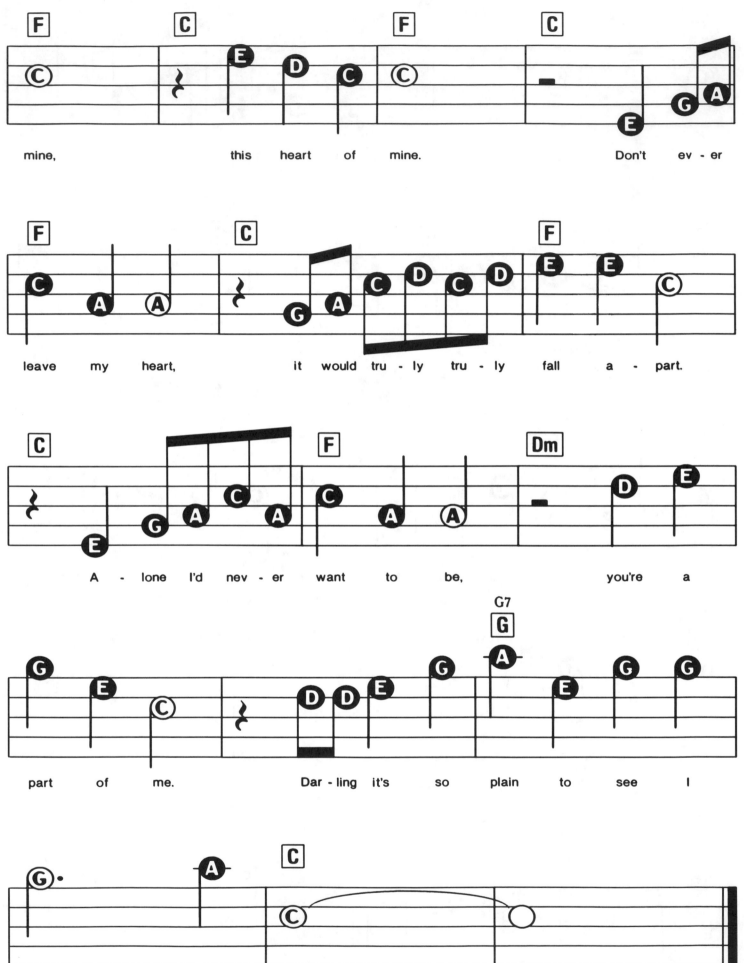

Wonderland By Night

Registration 9
Rhythm: Slow Rock or Ballad

Words by Lincoln Chase
Music by Klauss-Gunter Neuman

144

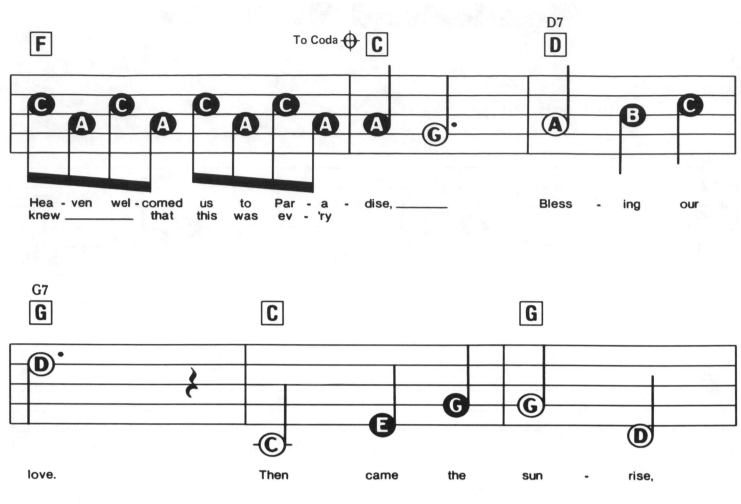

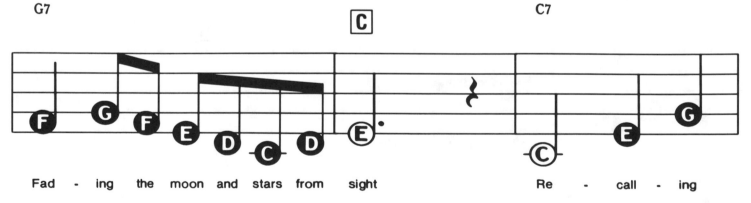

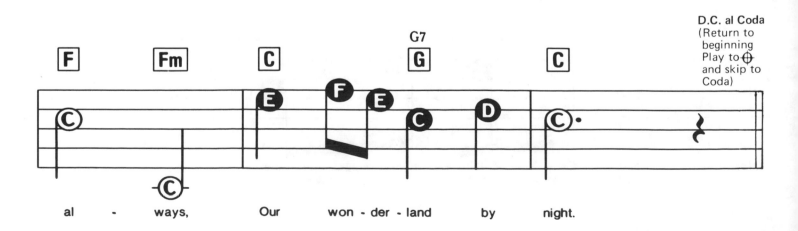

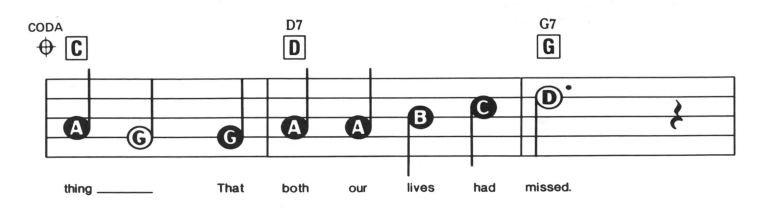

thing _____ That both our lives had missed.

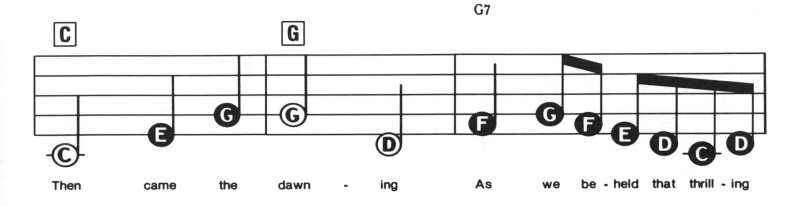

Then came the dawn - ing As we be - held that thrill - ing

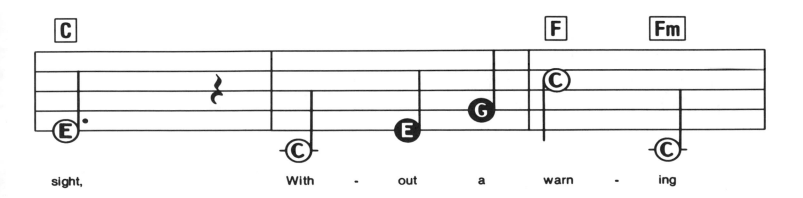

sight, With - out a warn - ing

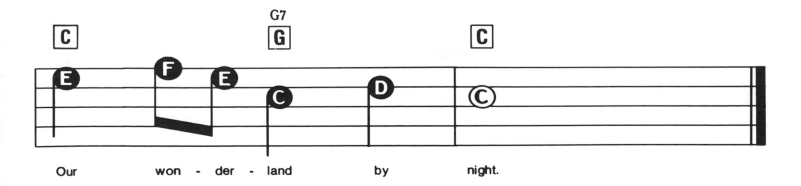

Our won - der - land by night.

Too Marvelous For Words

Registration 5
Rhythm: Swing or Jazz

Words by Johnny Mercer
Music by Richard A. Whiting

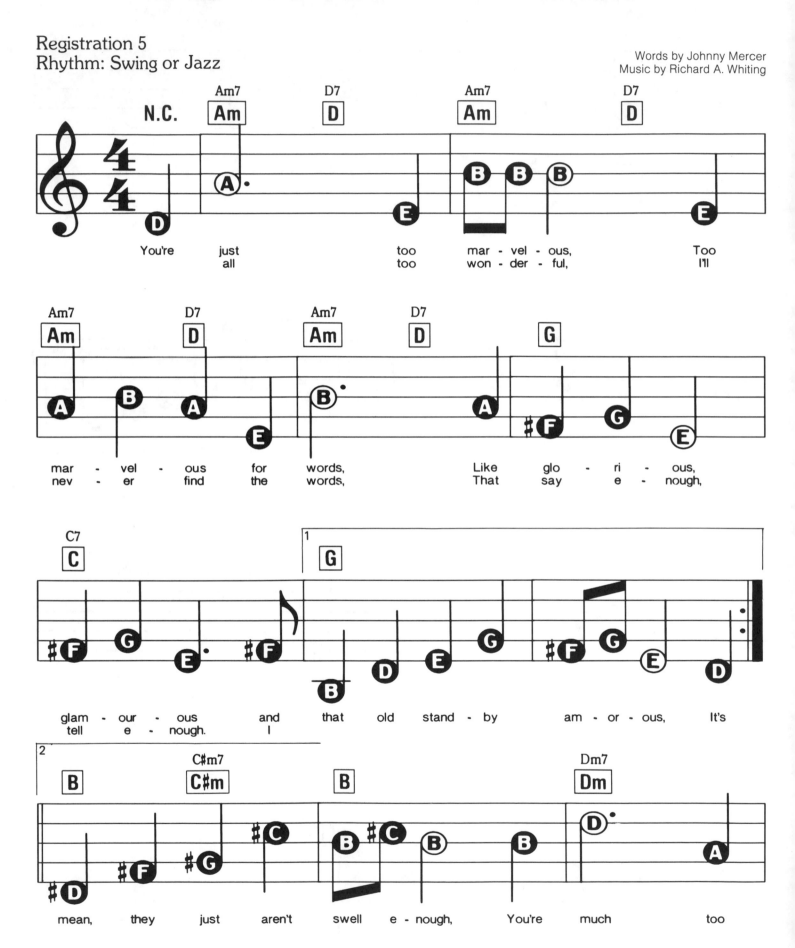

147

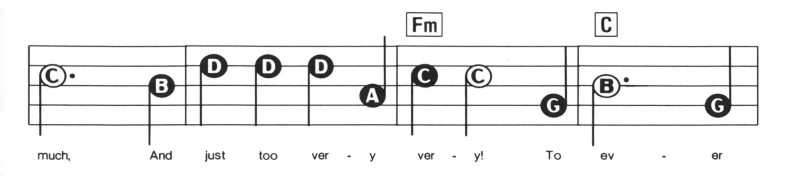

much, And just too ver - y ver - y! To ev - er

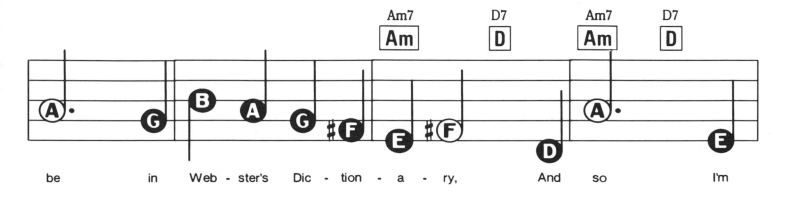

be in Web - ster's Dic - tion - a - ry, And so I'm

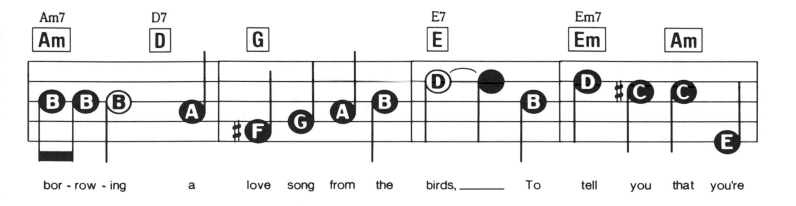

bor - row - ing a love song from the birds, _____ To tell you that you're

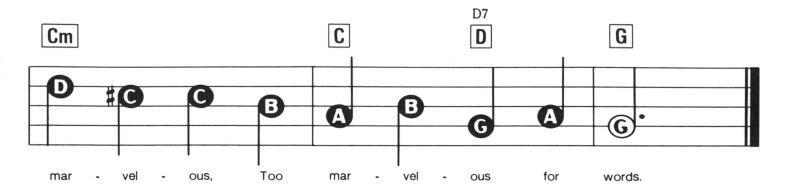

mar - vel - ous, Too mar - vel - ous for words.

Two Hearts In 3/4 Time
(Zwei Herzen Im Dreivierteltakt)

Registration 3
Rhythm: Waltz

Words by W. Reisch and A. Robinson
English Translation by Joe Young
Music by Robert Stolz

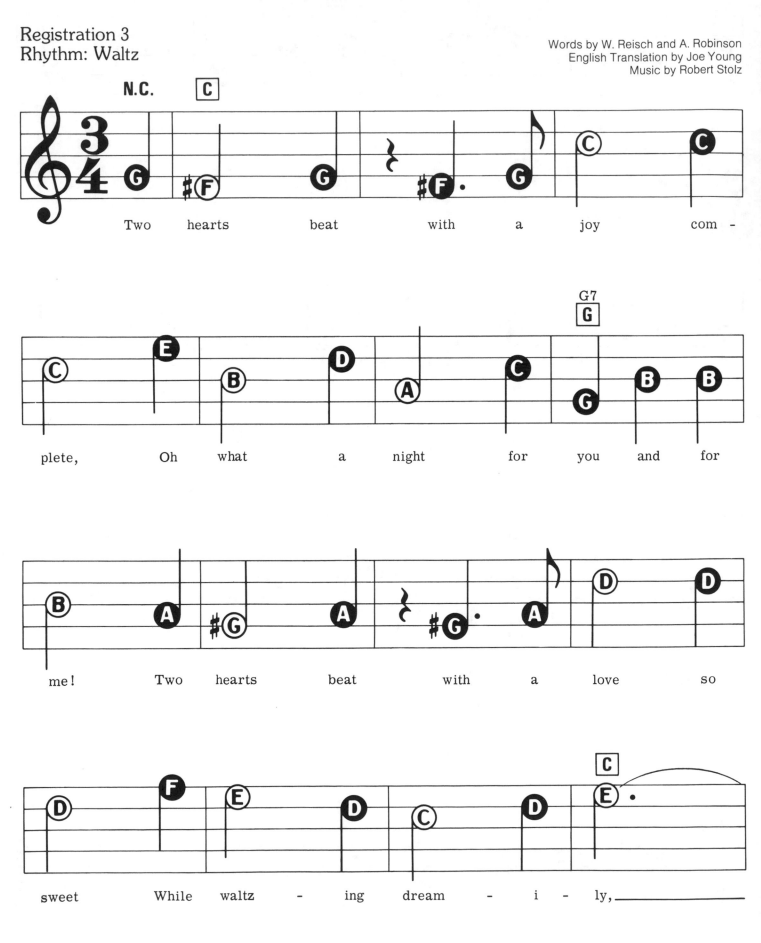

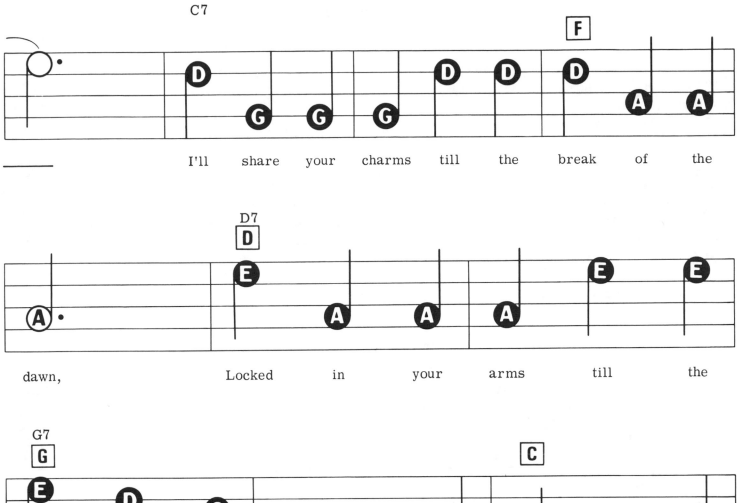

I'll   share   your   charms   till   the   break   of   the

dawn,   Locked   in   your   arms   till   the

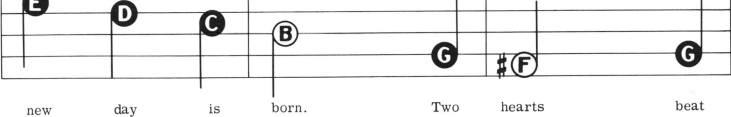

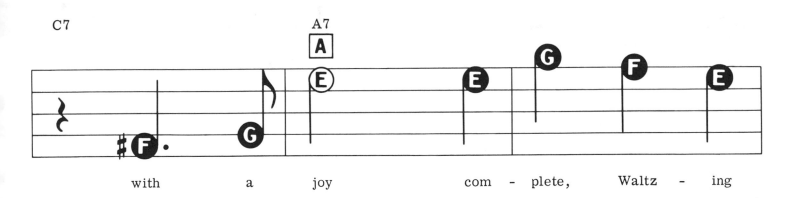

new   day   is   born.   Two   hearts   beat

with   a   joy   com - plete,   Waltz - ing

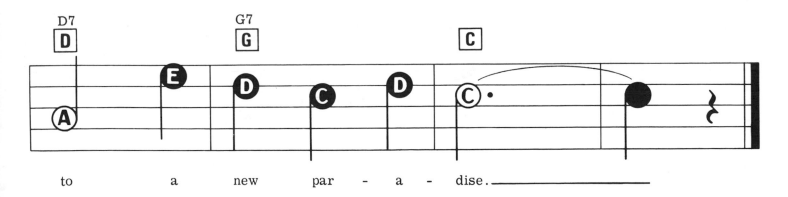

to   a   new   par - a - dise._____

Wanted

Registration 4
Rhythm: Ballad

Words and Music by
Jack Fulton & Lois Steele

151

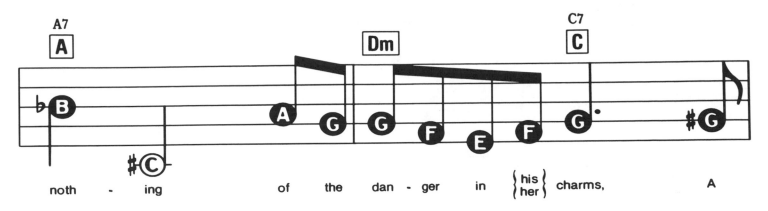

noth - ing   of the dan - ger in {his}{her} charms,   A

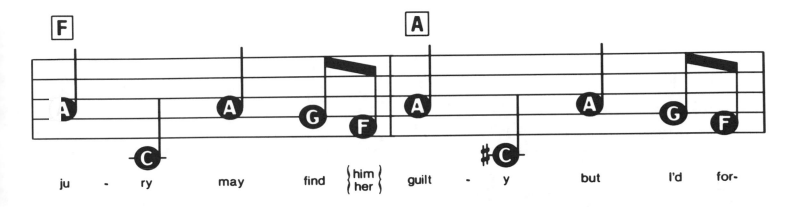

ju - ry may find {him}{her} guilt - y but I'd for-

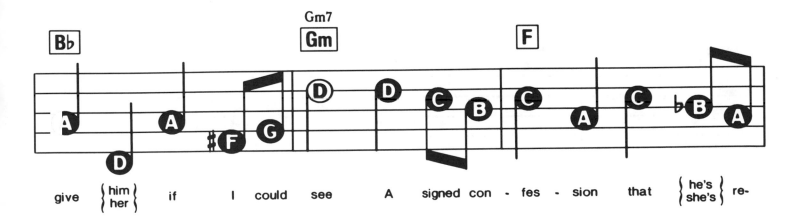

give {him}{her} if I could see A signed con - fes - sion that {he's}{she's} re-

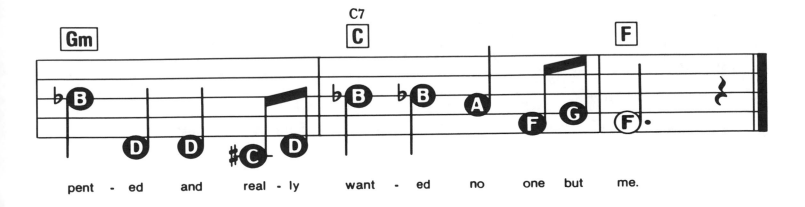

pent - ed and real - ly want - ed no one but me.

You Do Something To Me

Registration 4
Rhythm: Fox Trot or Swing

Words and Music by
Cole Porter

153

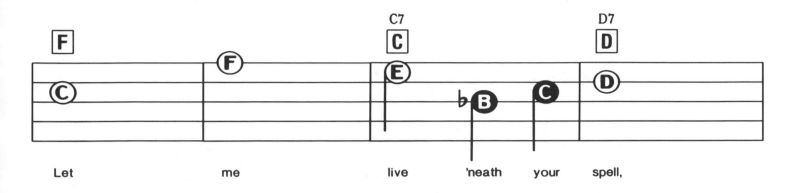

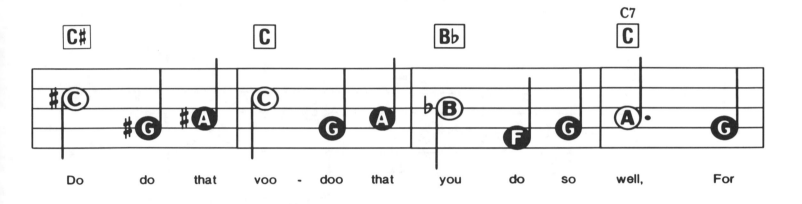

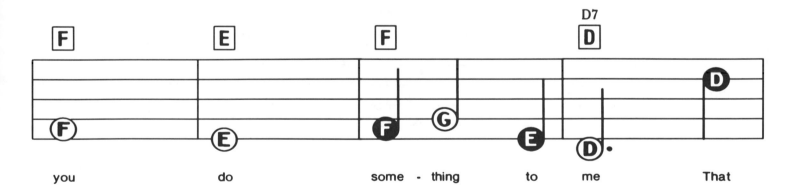

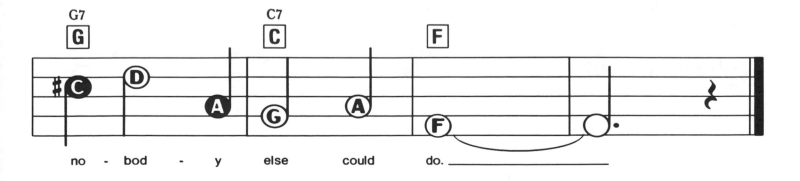

You're An Old Smoothie

("Take A Chance")

Registration 4
Rhythm: Fox Trot or Swing

Words by B.G. DeSylva
Music by Richard A. Whiting and Herb Brown Nacio

You're an old smooth - ie, I'm an old
You're an old mean - ie, I'm a big

soft - ie; I'm just like put - ty in the hands of a
boob - ie, I just go nut - ty, in the hands of a

girl like you.
girl like you. Poor me, you

played me for a sap; Poor you, you thought you'd laid a trap!

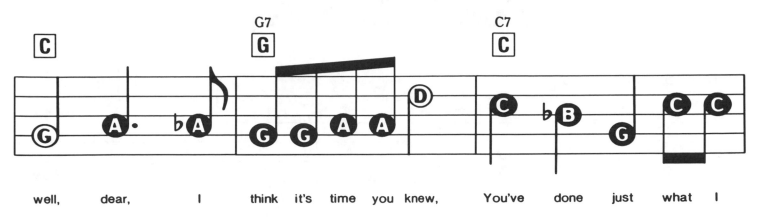

well, dear, I think it's time you knew, You've done just what I

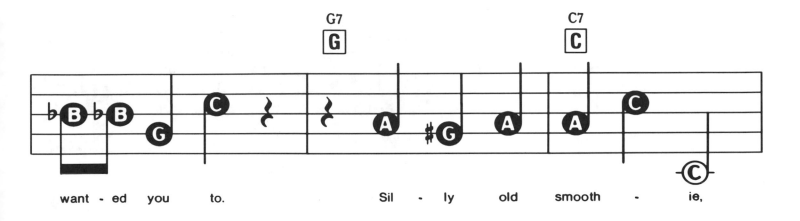

want - ed you to. Sil - ly old smooth - ie,

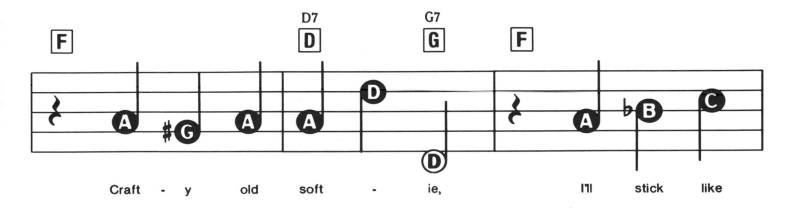

Craft - y old soft - ie, I'll stick like

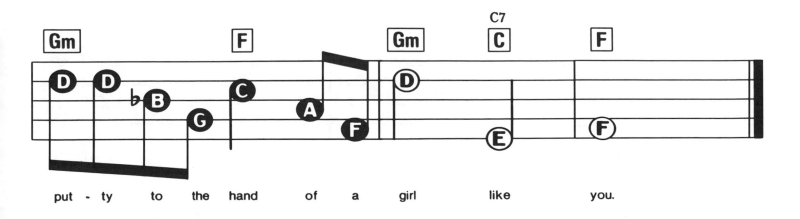

put - ty to the hand of a girl like you.

You're The Top

Registration 4
Rhythm: Swing or Jazz

Words and Music by
Cole Porter

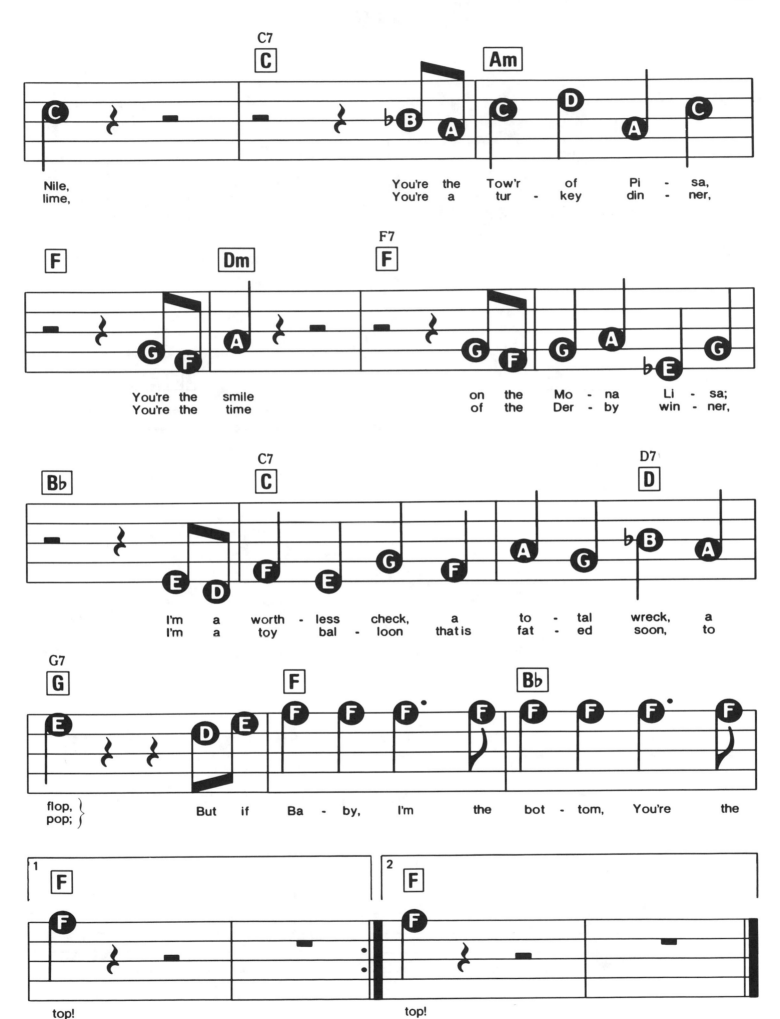

Nile,
lime,

You're the Tow'r of Pi - sa,
You're a tur - key din - ner,

You're the smile
You're the time

on the Mo - na Li - sa;
of the Der - by win - ner,

I'm a worth - less check, a to - tal wreck, a
I'm a toy bal - loon that is fat - ed soon, to

flop, }
pop; }

But if Ba - by, I'm the bot - tom, You're the

top!

top!

Zigeuner

Registration 5
Rhythm: Waltz

Words and Music by
Noel Coward

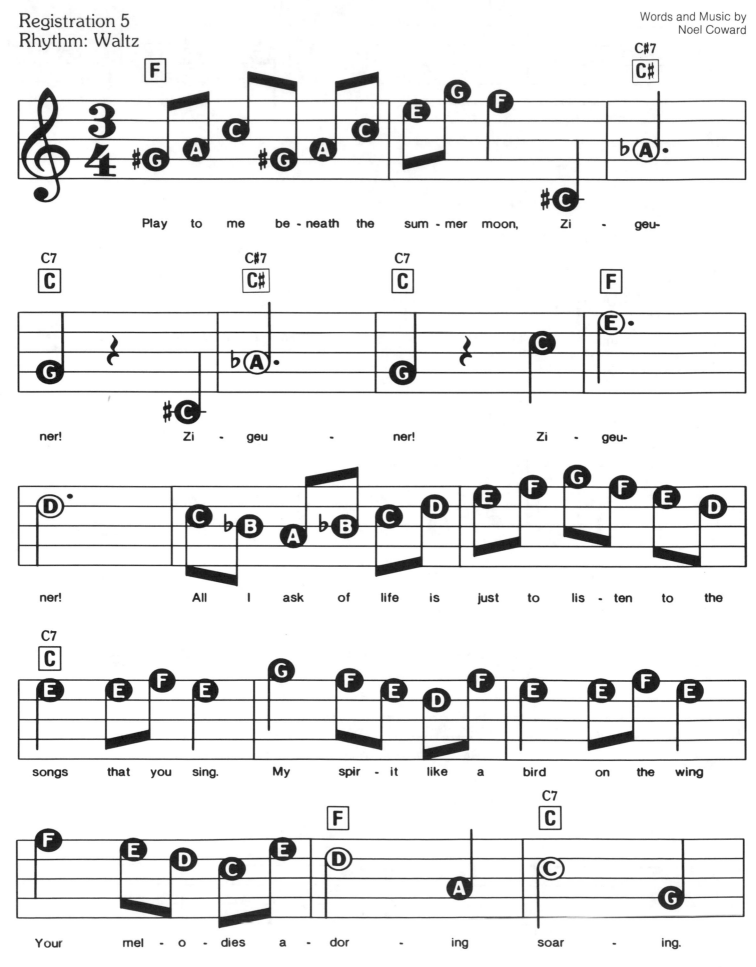

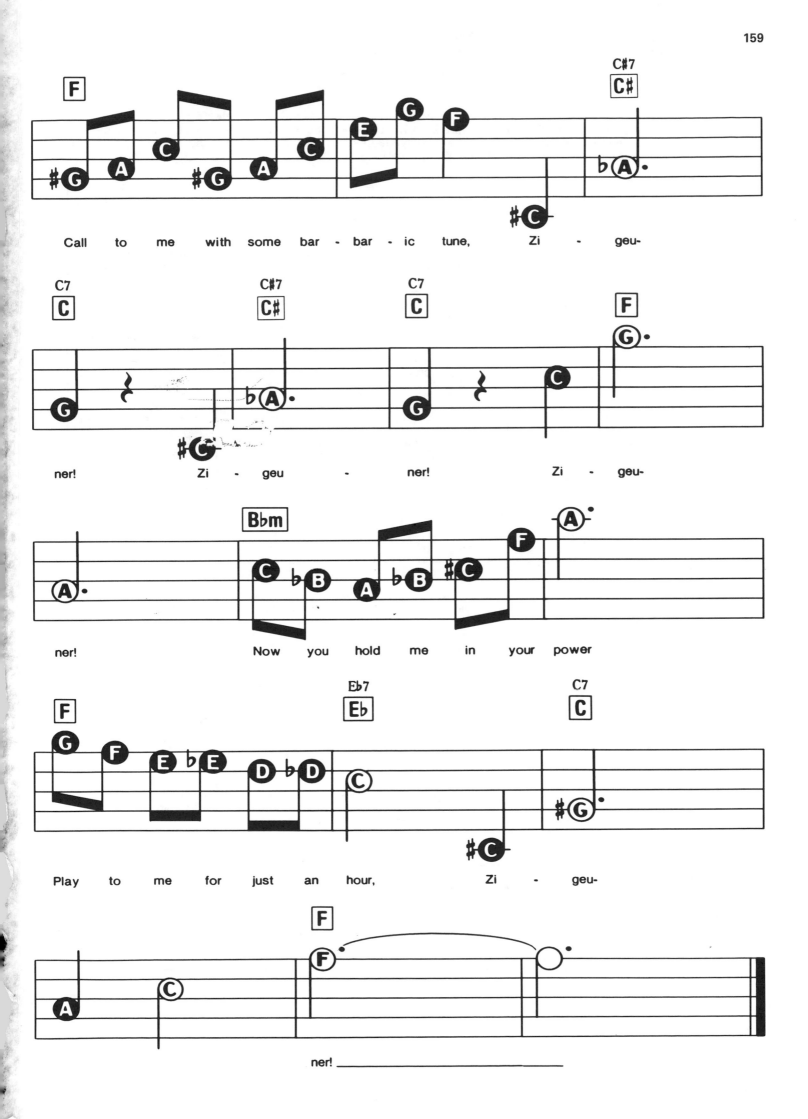

Call to me with some bar - bar - ic tune, Zi - geu-

ner! Zi - geu - ner! Zi - geu-

ner! Now you hold me in your power

Play to me for just an hour, Zi - geu-

ner! _____

E-Z Play® TODAY Registration Guide
For All Organs

On the following chart are 10 numbered registrations for both tonebar (TB) and electronic tab organs. The numbers correspond to the registration numbers on the E-Z Play TODAY songs. Set up as many voices and controls listed for each specific number as you have available on your instrument. For more detailed registrations, ask your dealer for the E-Z Play TODAY Registration Guide for your particular organ model.

REG. NO.		UPPER (SOLO)	LOWER (ACCOMPANIMENT)	PEDAL	GENERALS
1	Tab	Flute 16', 2'	Diapason 8' Flute 4'	Flute 16', 8'	Tremolo/Leslie – Fast
	TB	80 0808 000	(00) 7600 000	46, Sustain	Tremolo/Leslie – Fast (Upper/Lower)
2	Tab	Flute 16', 8', 4', 2', 1'	Diapason 8' Flute 8', 4'	Flute 16' String 8'	Tremolo/Leslie – Fast
	TB	80 7806 004	(00) 7503 000	46, Sustain	Tremolo/Leslie – Fast (Upper/Lower)
3	Tab	Flute 8', 4', 2²⁄₃', 2' String 8', 4'	Diapason 8' Flute 4' String 8'	Flute 16', 8'	Tremolo/Leslie – Fast
	TB	40 4555 554	(00) 7503 333	46, Sustain	Tremolo/Leslie – Fast (Upper/Lower)
4	Tab	Flute 16', 8', 4' Reed 16', 8'	Flute 8', (4) Reed 8'	Flute 8' String 8'	Tremolo/Leslie – Fast
	TB	80 7766 008	(00) 7540 000	54, Sustain	Tremolo/Leslie – Fast (Upper/Lower)
5	Tab	Flute 16', 4', 2' Reed 16', 8' String 8', 4'	Diapason 8' Reed 8' String 4'	Flute 16', 8' String 8'	Tremolo/Leslie
	TB	40 4555 554 Add all 4', 2' voices	(00) 7503 333	57, Sustain	
6	Tab	Flute 16', 8', 4' Diapason 8' String 8'	Diapason 8' Flute 8' String 4'	Diapason 8' Flute 8'	Tremolo/Leslie – Slow (Chorale)
	TB	45 6777 643	(00) 6604 020	64, Sustain	Tremolo/Leslie – Slow (Chorale)
7	Tab	Flute 16', 8', 5⅓', 2²⁄₃', 1'	Flute 8', 4' Reed 8'	Flute 8' String 8'	Chorus (optional) Perc Attack
	TB	88 0088 000	(00) 4333 000	45, Sustain	Tremolo/Leslie – Slow (Chorale)
8	Tab	Piano Preset or Flute 8' or Diapason 8'	Diapason 8'	Flute 8'	
	TB	00 8421 000	(00) 4302 010	43, Sustain	Perc Piano
9	Tab	Clarinet Preset or Flute 8' Reed 16', 8'	Flute 8' Reed 8'	Flute 16', 8'	Vibrato
	TB	00 8080 840	(00) 5442 000	43, Sustain	Vibrato
10	Tab	String (Violin) Preset or Flute 16' String 8', 4'	Flute 8' Reed 8'	Flute 16', 8'	Vibrato or Delayed Vibrato
	TB	00 7888 888	(00) 7765 443	57, Sustain	Vibrato or Delayed Vibrato

NOTE: TIBIAS may be used in place of FLUTES.
VIBRATO may be used in place of LESLIE.